West's Law School Advisory Board

STATUTORY SUPPLEMENT TO
EMPLOYMENT DISCRIMINATION LAW

CASES AND MATERIALS ON EQUALITY IN THE WORKPLACE

Eighth Edition

By

Dianne Avery
Professor of Law
University at Buffalo Law School
The State University of New York

Maria L. Ontiveros
Professor of Law
University of San Francisco School of Law

Roberto L. Corrada
Professor of Law
University of Denver Sturm College of Law

Michael Selmi
Samuel Tyler Research Professor of Law
The George Washington University Law School

Melissa Hart
Associate Professor of Law
University of Colorado Law School

for
THE LABOR LAW GROUP

AMERICAN CASEBOOK SERIES®

WEST®

A Thomson Reuters business

Mat #41059613

Printed in the United States of America

ISBN: 978–0–314–26731–3

Table of Contents

STATUTORY SUPPLEMENT TO

EMPLOYMENT DISCRIMINATION LAW

CASES AND MATERIALS ON EQUALITY IN THE WORKPLACE

Eighth Edition

CONSTITUTION OF THE UNITED STATES OF AMERICA

FIFTH AMENDMENT [1791]

No person shall be * * * deprived of life, liberty, or property, without due process of law * * *.

THIRTEENTH AMENDMENT [1865]

Section 1. Neither slavery nor involuntary servitude, except as a punishment for crime whereof the party shall have been duly convicted, shall exist within the United States, or any place subject to their jurisdiction.

Section 2. Congress shall have power to enforce this article by appropriate legislation.

FOURTEENTH AMENDMENT [1868]

Section 1. All persons born or naturalized in the United States, and subject to the jurisdiction thereof, are citizens of the United States and of the State wherein they reside. No State shall make or enforce any law which shall abridge the privileges or immunities of citizens of the United States; nor shall any State deprive any person of life, liberty, or property, without due process of law; nor deny to any person within its jurisdiction the equal protection of the laws.

* * *

Section 5. The Congress shall have power to enforce, by appropriate legislation, the provisions of this article.

CIVIL RIGHTS ACT OF 1866
42 U.S.C. §§ 1981 and 1981a

42 U.S.C. § 1981. Equal rights under the law.[1]

(a) All persons within the jurisdiction of the United States shall have the same right in every State and Territory to make and enforce contracts, to sue, be parties, give evidence, and to the full and equal benefit of all laws and proceedings for the security of persons and property as is enjoyed by white citizens, and shall be subject to like punishment, pains, penalties, taxes, licenses, and exactions of every kind, and to no other.

(b) For purposes of this section, the term "make and enforce contracts" includes the making, performance, modification, and termination of contracts, and the enjoyment of all benefits, privileges, terms and conditions of the contractual relationship.

(c) The rights protected by this section are protected against impairment by nongovernmental discrimination and impairment under color of State law.

42 U.S.C. § 1981a. Damages in cases of intentional discrimination in employment

(a) Right of recovery

(1) Civil rights

In an action brought by a complaining party under section 706 or 717 of the Civil Rights Act of 1964 [42 U.S.C. § 2000e–5 or 2000e–16] against a respondent who engaged in unlawful intentional discrimination (not an employment practice that is unlawful because of its disparate impact) prohibited under section 703, 704, or 717 of the Act [42 U.S.C. § 2000e–2, 2000e–3, or 2000e–16], and provided that the complaining party cannot recover under section 1981 of this title, the complaining party may recover compensatory and punitive damages as allowed in subsection (b) of this section, in addition to any relief authorized by section 706(g) of the Civil Rights Act of 1964, from the respondent

(2) Disability

In an action brought by a complaining party under the powers, remedies, and procedures set forth in section 706 or 717

1. Derived from § 1 of the Civil Rights Act of 1866, and §§ 16 and 18 of the Civil Rights Act of 1870. In the 1874 revision of the United States Code, § 1981 was codified as § 1977. 18 Stat. 348. Amended by the Civil Rights Act of 1991. Pub.L.No. 102–166, 105 Stat. 1071 (1991). The 1991 amendments are in boldface.

of the Civil Rights Act of 1964 [42 U.S.C. § 2000e–5 or 2000e–16] (as provided in section 107(a) of the Americans with Disabilities Act of 1990 [42 U.S.C. § 12117(a)], and section 794a (a)(1) of title 29 [the Rehabilitation Act of 1973] respectively) against a respondent who engaged in unlawful intentional discrimination (not an employment practice that is unlawful because of its disparate impact) under section 791 of title 29 [the Rehabilitation Act of 1973] and the regulations implementing section 791 of title 29, or who violated the requirements of section 791 of title 29 or the regulations implementing section 791 of title 29 concerning the provisions of a reasonable accommodation, or section 102 of the Americans with Disabilities Act of 1990 [42 U.S.C. § 12112], or committed a violation of section 102(b)(5) of the Act, against an individual, the complaining party may recover compensatory and punitive damages as allowed in subsection (b) of this section, in addition to any relief authorized by section 706(g) of the Civil Rights Act of 1964, from the respondent.

(3) Reasonable accommodation and good faith effort

In cases where a discriminatory practice involves the provision of a reasonable accommodation pursuant to section 102(b)(5) of the Americans with Disabilities Act of 1990 [42 U.S.C. § 12112(b)(5)] or regulations implementing section 791 of title 29, damages may not be awarded under this section where the covered entity demonstrates good faith efforts, in consultation with the person with the disability who has informed the covered entity that accommodation is needed, to identify and make a reasonable accommodation that would provide such individual with an equally effective opportunity and would not cause an undue hardship on the operation of the business.

(b) Compensatory and punitive damages

(1) Determination of punitive damages

A complaining party may recover punitive damages under this section against a respondent (other than a government, government agency or political subdivision) if the complaining party demonstrates that the respondent engaged in a discriminatory practice or discriminatory practices with malice or with reckless indifference to the federally protected rights of an aggrieved individual.

(2) Exclusions from compensatory damages

Compensatory damages awarded under this section shall not include backpay, interest on backpay, or any other type of relief authorized under section 706(g) of the Civil Rights Act of 1964 [42 U.S.C. § 2000e–5(g)].

(3) Limitations

The sum of the amount of compensatory damages awarded under this section for future pecuniary losses, emotional pain, suffering, inconvenience, mental anguish, loss of enjoyment of life, and other nonpecuniary losses, and the amount of punitive damages awarded under this section, shall not exceed, for each complaining party—

(A) in the case of a respondent who has more than 14 and fewer than 101 employees in each of 20 or more calendar weeks in the current or preceding calendar year, $50,000;

(B) in the case of a respondent who has more than 100 and fewer than 201 employees in each of 20 or more calendar weeks in the current or preceding calendar year, $100,000; and

(C) in the case of a respondent who has more than 200 and fewer than 501 employees in each of 20 or more calendar weeks in the current or preceding calendar year, $200,000; and

(D) in the case of a respondent who has more than 500 employees in each of 20 or more calendar weeks in the current or preceding calendar year, $300,000.

(4) Construction

Nothing in this section shall be construed to limit the scope of, or the relief available under, section 1981 of this title.

(c) Jury Trial

If a complaining party seeks compensatory or punitive damages under this section—

(1) any party may demand a trial by jury; and

(2) the court shall not inform the jury of the limitations described in subsection (b)(3) of this section.

(d) Definitions

As used in this section:

(1) Complaining party

The term "complaining party" means—

(A) in the case of a person seeking to bring an action under subsection (a)(1) of this section, the Equal Employment Opportunity Commission, the Attorney General, or a person who may bring an action or proceeding under title VII of the Civil Rights Act of 1964 [42 U.S.C. § 2000e et seq.]; or

(B) in the case of a person seeking to bring an action under subsection (a)(2) of this section, the Equal Employment Opportunity Commission, the Attorney General, a person who may bring an action or proceeding under section 794a (a)(1) of title 29 [the Rehabilitation Act of 1973], or a person who may bring an action or proceeding under title I of the Americans with Disabilities Act of 1990 [42 U.S.C. § 12171 et seq.].

(2) Discriminatory practice

The term "discriminatory practice" means the discrimination described in paragraph (1), or the discrimination or the violation described in paragraph (2), of subsection (a) of this section.

CIVIL RIGHTS ACT OF 1871
42 U.S.C. § 1983

Civil action for deprivation of rights[1]

Every person who, under color of any statute, ordinance, regulation, custom, or usage, of any State or Territory or the District of Columbia, subjects, or causes to be subjected, any citizen of the United States or other persons within the jurisdiction thereof to the deprivation of any rights, privileges or immunities secured by the Constitution and laws, shall be liable to the person injured in an action at law, suit in equity, or other proper proceedings for redress. For purposes of this section, any Act of Congress applicable exclusively to the District of Columbia shall be considered to be a statute of the District of Columbia.

1. Derived from § 1 of the Civil Rights Act of 1871. 17 Stat. 13. Codified as § 1979 of the Revised Statutes. 18 Stat. 348.

CIVIL RIGHTS ATTORNEY'S FEES AWARD ACT OF 1976
42 U.S.C. § 1988

Proceedings in vindication of civil rights; attorney's fees

* * *

(b) Attorney's fees

In any action or proceeding to enforce a provision of sections 1981, 1981a, 1982, 1983, and 1986 of this title, title IX of Public Law 92–318 [20 U.S.C. § 1681 et seq.], the Religious Freedom Restoration Act of 1993 [42 U.S.C. § 2000bb et seq.], or section 13981 of this title, the court, in its discretion, may allow the prevailing party, other than the United States, a reasonable attorney's fee as part of the costs.

(c) Expert Fees

In awarding an attorney's fee under subsection (b) in any action or proceeding to enforce a provision of section 1981a, the court, in its discretion, may include expert fees as part of the attorney's fee.[1]

1. Section (c) was added to § 1988 pursuant to the Civil Rights Act of 1991. Pub. L.No. 101–239, 105 Stat. 1071 (1991).

EQUAL PAY ACT OF 1963
29 U.S.C. § 206(d)

(d) Prohibition of sex discrimination

(1) No employer having employees subject to any provisions of this section shall discriminate, within any establishment in which such employees are employed, between employees on the basis of sex by paying wages to employees in such establishment at a rate less than the rate at which he pays wages to employees of the opposite sex in such establishment for equal work on jobs the performance of which requires equal skill, effort, and responsibility, and which are performed under similar working conditions, except where such payment is made pursuant to (i) a seniority system; (ii) a merit system; (iii) a system which measures earnings by quantity or quality of production; or (iv) a differential based on any other factor other than sex: *Provided*, That an employer who is paying a wage rate differential in violation of this subsection shall not, in order to comply with the provisions of this subsection, reduce the wage rate of any employee.

(2) No labor organization, or its agents, representing employees of an employer having employees subject to any provisions of this section shall cause or attempt to cause such an employer to discriminate against an employee in violation of paragraph (1) of this subsection.

(3) For purposes of administration and enforcement, any amounts owing to any employee which have been withheld in violation of this subsection shall be deemed to be unpaid minimum wages or unpaid overtime compensation under this chapter.

(4) As used in this subsection, the term "labor organization" means any organization of any kind, or any agency or employee representation committee or plan, in which employees participate and which exists for the purpose, in whole or in part, of dealing with employers concerning grievances, labor disputes, wages, rates of pay, hours of employment, or conditions of work.

TITLE VII OF THE CIVIL RIGHTS ACT OF 1964[1]
42 U.S.C. §§ 2000e—2000e–17

Sec. 701 [42 U.S.C. § 2000e]. Definitions

For the purposes of this subchapter—

(a) The term "person" includes one or more individuals, *governments, governmental agencies, political subdivisions*, labor unions, partnerships, associations, corporations, legal representatives, mutual companies, joint-stock companies, trusts, unincorporated organizations, trustees, trustees in cases under title 11, or receivers.

(b) The term "employer" means a person engaged in an industry affecting commerce who has *fifteen* or more employees for each working day in each of twenty or more calendar weeks in the current or preceding calendar year, and any agent of such a person, but such term does not include (1) the United States, a corporation wholly owned by the Government of the United States, an Indian tribe, or *any department or agency of the District of Columbia subject by statute to procedures of the competitive service (as defined in section 2102 of title 5)*, or (2) a bona fide private membership club (other than a labor organization) which is exempt from taxation under section 501(c) of title 26, *except that during the first year after March 24, 1972*, persons having fewer than *twenty-five* employees (and their agents) shall not be considered *employers*.

(c) The term "employment agency" means any person regularly undertaking with or without compensation to procure employees for an employer or to procure for employees opportunities to work for an employer and includes an agent of such a person.

(d) The term "labor organization" means a labor organization engaged in an industry affecting commerce, and any agent of such an organization, and includes any organization of any kind, any agency, or employee representation committee, group, association, or plan so engaged in which employees participate and which exists for the purpose, in whole or in part, of dealing with employers concerning grievances, labor disputes, wages, rates of pay, hours, or other terms or conditions of employment, and any conference, general committee, joint or system board, or joint council so engaged which is subordinate to a national or international labor organization.

(e) A labor organization shall be deemed to be engaged in an industry affecting commerce if (1) it maintains or operates a hiring hall

1. The provisions of Title VII, as originally enacted, are in roman type; the 1972 amendments are printed in italics; the 1978 amendment in § 701(k) and the amendments by the Lilly Ledbetter Fair Pay Act of 2009 in § 706(e) are in boldface italics; and the amendments added by the Civil Rights Act of 1991 are printed in boldface type.

or hiring office which procures employees for an employer or procures for employees opportunities to work for an employer, or (2) the number of its members (or, where it is a labor organization composed of other labor organizations or their representatives, if the aggregate number of the members of such other labor organization) is (A) *twenty-five or more during the first year after March 24, 1972, or (B) fifteen or more thereafter*, and such labor organization—

(1) is the certified representative of employees under the provisions of the National Labor Relations Act, as amended [29 U.S.C. § 151 et seq.], or the Railway Labor Act, as amended [45 U.S.C. § 151 et seq.];

(2) although not certified, is a national or international labor organization or a local labor organization recognized or acting as the representative of employees of an employer or employers engaged in an industry affecting commerce; or

(3) has chartered a local labor organization or subsidiary body which is representing or actively seeking to represent employees of employers within the meaning of paragraph (1) or (2); or

(4) has been chartered by a labor organization representing or actively seeking to represent employees within the meaning of paragraph (1) or (2) as the local or subordinate body through which such employees may enjoy membership or become affiliated with such labor organization; or

(5) is a conference, general committee, joint or system board, or joint council subordinate to a national or international labor organization, which includes a labor organization engaged in an industry affecting commerce within the meaning of any of the preceding paragraphs of this subsection.

(f) The term "employee" means an individual employed by an employer, *except that the term "employee" shall not include any person elected to public office in any State or political subdivision of any State by the qualified voters thereof, or any person chosen by such officer to be on such officer's personal staff, or an appointee on the policy making level or an immediate adviser with respect to the exercise of the constitutional or legal powers of the office. The exemption set forth in the preceding sentence shall not include employees subject to the civil service laws of a State government, governmental agency or political subdivision.* **With respect to employment in a foreign country, such term includes an individual who is a citizen of the United States.**

(g) The term "commerce" means trade, traffic, commerce, transportation, transmission, or communication among the several States; or between a State and any place outside thereof; or within the District of Columbia, or a possession of the United States; or between points in the same State but through a point outside thereof.

(h) The term "industry affecting commerce" means any activity, business, or industry in commerce or in which a labor dispute would hinder or obstruct commerce or the free flow of commerce and includes any activity or industry "affecting commerce" within the meaning of the Labor–Management Reporting and Disclosure Act of 1959 [29 U.S.C. § 401 et seq.] *and further includes any governmental industry, business, or activity.*

(i) The term "State" includes a State of the United States, the District of Columbia, Puerto Rico, the Virgin Islands, American Samoa, Guam, Wake Island, the Canal Zone, and Outer Continental Shelf lands defined in the Outer Continental Shelf Lands Act [43 U.S.C. § 1331 et seq.].

(j) *The term "religion" includes all aspects of religious observance and practice, as well as belief, unless an employer demonstrates that he is unable to reasonably accommodate to an employee's or prospective employee's religious observance or practice without undue hardship on the conduct of the employer's business.*

(k) *The terms "because of sex" or "on the basis of sex" include, but are not limited to, because of or on the basis of pregnancy, childbirth, or related medical conditions; and women affected by pregnancy, childbirth, or related medical conditions shall be treated the same for all employment-related purposes, including receipt of benefits under fringe benefit programs, as other persons not so affected but similar in their ability or inability to work, and nothing in section 2000e–2(h) of this subchapter shall be interpreted to permit otherwise. This subsection shall not require an employer to pay for health insurance benefits for abortion, except where the life of the mother would be endangered if the fetus were carried to term, or except where medical complications have arisen from an abortion: Provided, That nothing herein shall preclude an employer from providing abortion benefits or otherwise affect bargaining agreements in regard to abortion.*

(*l*) The term "complaining party" means the Commission, the Attorney General, or a person who may bring an action or proceeding under this subchapter.

(m) The term "demonstrates" means meets the burdens of production and persuasion.

(n) The term "respondent" means an employer, employment agency, labor organization, joint labor-management committee controlling apprenticeship or other training or retraining program, including an on-the-job training program, or Federal entity subject to section 2000e–16 of this title.

Sec. 702 [42 U.S.C. § 2000e–1]. Applicability to foreign and religious employment

(a) Inapplicability of subchapter to certain aliens and employees of religious entities

This subchapter shall not apply to an employer with respect to the employment of aliens outside any State, or to a religious corporation, association, *educational institution*, or society with respect to the employment of individuals of a particular religion to perform work connected with the carrying on by such corporation, association, *educational institution, or society of its activities.*

(b) Compliance with statute as violative of foreign law

It shall not be unlawful under section 2000e–2 or 2000e–3 for an employer (or a corporation controlled by an employer), labor organization, employment agency, or joint labor-management committee controlling apprenticeship or other training or retraining (including on-the-job training programs) to take any action otherwise prohibited by such section, with respect to an employee in a workplace in a foreign country if compliance with such section would cause such employer (or such corporation), such organization, such agency, or such committee to violate the law of the foreign country in which such workplace is located.

(c) Control of corporation incorporated in foreign country

(1) If an employer controls a corporation whose place of incorporation is a foreign country, any practice prohibited by section 2000e–2 or 2000e–3 of this title engaged in by such corporation shall be presumed to be engaged in by such employer.

(2) Sections 2000e–2 and 2000e–3 of this title shall not apply with respect to the foreign operations of an employer that is a foreign person not controlled by an American employer.

(3) For purposes of this subsection, the determination of whether an employer controls a corporation shall be based on—

(A) the interrelation of operations;

(B) the common management;

(C) the centralized control of labor relations; and

(D) the common ownership or financial control, of the employer and the corporation.

Sec. 703 [42 U.S.C. § 2000e–2]. Unlawful employment practices

(a) Employer practices

It shall be an unlawful employment practice for an employer—

(1) to fail or refuse to hire or to discharge any individual, or otherwise to discriminate against any individual with respect to his compensation, terms, conditions, or privileges of employment, because of such individual's race, color, religion, sex, or national origin; or

(2) to limit, segregate, or classify his employees *or applicants for employment* in any way which would deprive or tend to deprive any individual of employment opportunities or otherwise adversely affect his

status as an employee, because of such individual's race, color, religion, sex, or national origin.

(b) Employment agency practices

It shall be an unlawful employment practice for an employment agency to fail or refuse to refer for employment, or otherwise to discriminate against, any individual because of his race, color, religion, sex, or national origin, or to classify or refer for employment any individual on the basis of his race, color, religion, sex, or national origin.

(c) Labor organization practices

It shall be an unlawful employment practice for a labor organization—

(1) to exclude or to expel from its membership, or otherwise to discriminate against, any individual because of his race, color, religion, sex, or national origin;

(2) to limit, segregate, or classify its membership *or applicants for membership*, or to classify or fail or refuse to refer for employment any individual, in any way which would deprive or tend to deprive any individual of employment opportunities, or would limit such employment opportunities or otherwise adversely affect his status as an employee or as an applicant for employment, because of such individual's race, color, religion, sex, or national origin; or

(3) to cause or attempt to cause an employer to discriminate against an individual in violation of this section.

(d) Training programs

It shall be an unlawful employment practice for any employer, labor organization, or joint labor-management committee controlling apprenticeship or other training or retraining, including on-the-job training programs to discriminate against any individual because of his race, color, religion, sex, or national origin in admission to, or employment in, any program established to provide apprenticeship or other training.

(e) Businesses or enterprises with personnel qualified on basis of religion, sex, or national origin; educational institutions with personnel of particular religion

Notwithstanding any other provision of this subchapter, (1) it shall not be an unlawful employment practice for an employer to hire and employ employees, for an employment agency to classify, or refer for employment any individual, for a labor organization to classify its membership or to classify or refer for employment any individual, or for an employer, labor organization, or joint labor-management committee controlling apprenticeship or other training or retraining programs to admit or employ any individual in any such program, on the basis of his religion, sex, or national origin in those certain instances where religion, sex, or national origin is a bona fide occupational qualification reasonably necessary to the normal operation of that particular business or enterprise, and (2) it shall not be an unlawful employment practice for a school, college, university, or other educational institution or institution of learning to hire and employ employees of a particular religion if such school, college, university, or other educational institution or institution of learning is, in whole or in substantial part, owned, supported, controlled, or managed by a particular religion or by a particular religious corporation, association, or society, or if the curriculum of such school, college, university, or other educational institution or institution of learning is directed toward the propagation of a particular religion.

(f) Members of Communist Party or Communist-action or Communist-front organizations

As used in this subchapter, the phrase "unlawful employment practice" shall not be deemed to include any action or measure taken by an employer, labor organization, joint labor-management committee, or employment agency with respect to an individual who is a member of the Communist Party of the United States or of any other organization required to register as a Communist-action or Communist-front organization by final order of the Subversive Activities Control Board pursuant to the Subversive Activities Control Act of 1950 [50 U.S.C. § 781 et seq.].

(g) National security

Notwithstanding any other provision of this subchapter, it shall not be an unlawful employment practice for an employer to fail or refuse to hire and employ any individual for any position, for an employer to discharge any individual from any position, or for an employment agency to fail or refuse to refer any individual for employment in any position, or for a labor organization to fail or refuse to refer any individual for employment in any position, if—

(1) the occupancy of such position, or access to the premises in or upon which any part of the duties of such position is performed or is to be performed, is subject to any requirement imposed in the interest of the national security of the United States under any security program in effect pursuant to or administered under any statute of the United States or any Executive order of the President; and

(2) such individual has not fulfilled or has ceased to fulfill that requirement.

(h) Seniority or merit system; quantity or quality of production; ability tests; compensation based on sex and authorized by minimum wage provisions

Notwithstanding any other provision of this subchapter, it shall not be an unlawful employment practice for an employer to apply different standards of compensation, or different terms, conditions, or privileges of employment pursuant to a bona fide seniority or merit system, or a system which measures earnings by quantity or quality of production or to employees who work in different locations, provided that such differences are not the result of an intention to discriminate because of race, color, religion, sex, or national origin, nor shall it be an unlawful employment practice for an employer to give and to act upon the results of any professionally developed ability test provided that such test, its administration or action upon the results is not designed, intended or used to discriminate because of race, color, religion, sex or national origin. It shall not be an unlawful employment practice under this subchapter for an employer to differentiate upon the basis of sex in determining the amount of the wages or compensation paid or to be paid to employees of such employer if such differentiation is authorized by the provisions of section 206(d) of title 29 [Equal Pay Act].

(i) Businesses or enterprises extending preferential treatment to Indians

Nothing contained in this subchapter shall apply to any business or enterprise on or near an Indian reservation with respect to any publicly announced employment practice of such business or enterprise under which a preferential treatment is given to any individual because he is an Indian living on or near a reservation.

(j) Preferential treatment not to be granted on account of existing number or percentage imbalance

Nothing contained in this subchapter shall be interpreted to require any employer, employment agency, labor organization, or joint labor-management committee subject to this subchapter to grant preferential treatment to any individual or to any group because of the race, color, religion, sex, or national origin of such individual or group on account of an imbalance which may exist with respect to the total number or percentage of persons of any race, color, religion, sex, or national origin employed by any employer, referred or classified for employment by any employment agency or labor organization, admitted to membership or classified by any labor organization, or admitted to, or employed in, any apprenticeship or other training program, in comparison with the total number or percentage of persons of such race, color, religion, sex, or national origin in any community, State, section, or other area, or in the available work force in any community, State, section, or other area.

(k) Burden of proof in disparate impact cases

(1)(A) An unlawful employment practice based on disparate impact is established under this subchapter only if—

(i) a complaining party demonstrates that a respondent uses a particular employment practice that causes a disparate impact on the basis of race, color, religion, sex, or national origin and the respondent fails to demonstrate that the challenged practice is job related for the position in question and consistent with business necessity; or

(ii) the complaining party makes the demonstration described in subparagraph (C) with respect to an alternative employment practice and the respondent refuses to adopt such alternative employment practice.

(B)(i) With respect to demonstrating that a particular employment practice causes a disparate impact as described in subparagraph (A)(i), the complaining party shall demonstrate that each particular challenged employment practice causes a disparate impact, except that if the complaining party can demonstrate to the court that the elements of a respondent's decisionmaking process are not capable of separation for analysis, the decisionmaking process may be analyzed as one employment practice.

(ii) If the respondent demonstrates that a specific employment practice does not cause the disparate impact, the respondent shall not be required to demonstrate that such practice is required by business necessity.

(C) The demonstration referred to by subparagraph (A)(ii) shall be in accordance with law as it existed on June 4, 1989, with respect to the concept of "alternative employment practice."[2]

(2) A demonstration that an employment practice is required by business necessity may not be used as a defense against a claim of intentional discrimination under this subchapter.

(3) Notwithstanding any other provision of this subchapter, a rule barring the employment of an individual who currently and knowingly uses or possesses a controlled substance, as defined in schedules I and II of section 102(6) of the Controlled Substances Act [21 U.S.C. § 802(6)], other than the use or possession of a drug taken under the supervision of a licensed health care professional, or any other use or possession authorized by the Controlled Substances Act [21 U.S.C. § 801 et seq.] or any other provision of Federal law, shall be considered an unlawful employment practice under this subchapter only if such rule is adopted or applied with an intent to discriminate because of race, color, religion, sex, or national origin.

(*l*) Prohibition of discriminatory use of test scores

It shall be an unlawful employment practice for a respondent, in connection with the selection or referral of applicants

2. Section 105(b) of the Civil Rights Act of 1991, Pub.L.No. 102–166, 105 Stat. 1071 (1991), provides that,

(b) No statements other than the interpretive memorandum appearing at Vol. 137 Congressional Record S15276 (daily ed. Oct. 25, 1991) shall be considered legislative history of, or relied upon in any way as legislative history in construing or applying, any provision of this Act that relates to Wards Cove— Business necessity/cumulation/ alternative business practice.

or candidates for employment or promotion, to adjust the scores of, use different cutoff scores for, or otherwise alter the results of, employment related tests on the basis of race, color, religion, sex, or national origin.

(m) Impermissible consideration of race, color, religion, sex or national origin in employment practices

Except as otherwise provided in this subchapter, an unlawful employment practice is established when the complaining party demonstrates that race, color, religion, sex, or national origin was a motivating factor for any employment practice, even though other factors also motivated the practice.

(n) Resolution of challenges to employment practices implementing litigated or consent judgments or orders

(1)(A) Notwithstanding any other provision of law, and except as provided in paragraph (2), an employment practice that implements and is within the scope of a litigated or consent judgment or order that resolves a claim of employment discrimination under the Constitution or Federal civil rights laws may not be challenged under the circumstances described in subparagraph (B).

(B) A practice described in subparagraph (A) may not be challenged in a claim under the Constitution or Federal civil rights laws

(i) by a person who, prior to the entry of the judgment or order described in subparagraph (A), had—

(I) actual notice of the proposed judgment or order sufficient to apprise such person that such judgment or order might adversely affect the interests and legal rights of such person and that an opportunity was available to present objections to such judgment or order by a future date certain; and

(II) a reasonable opportunity to present objections to such judgment or order; or

(ii) by a person whose interests were adequately represented by another person who had previously challenged the judgment or order on the same legal grounds and with a similar factual situation, unless there has been an intervening change in law or fact.

(2) Nothing in this subsection shall be construed to—

(A) alter the standards for intervention under rule 24 of the Federal Rules of Civil Procedure or apply to the rights of parties who have successfully intervened pursuant to such rule in the proceeding in which the parties intervened;

(B) apply to the rights of parties to the action in which a litigated or consent judgment or order was entered, or of members of a class represented or sought to be represented in such action, or of members of a group on whose behalf relief was sought in such action by the Federal Government;

(C) prevent challenges to a litigated or consent judgment or order on the ground that such judgment or order was obtained through collusion or fraud, or is transparently invalid or was entered by a court lacking subject matter jurisdiction; or

(D) authorize or permit the denial to any person of the due process of law required by the Constitution.

(3) Any action not precluded under this subsection that challenges an employment consent judgment or order described in paragraph (1) shall be brought in the court, and if possible before the judge, that entered such judgment or order. Nothing in this subsection shall preclude a transfer of such action pursuant to section 1404 of Title 28.

Sec. 704 [42 U.S.C. § 2000e–3]. Other Unlawful Employment Practices

(a) Discrimination for making charges, testifying, assisting, or participating in enforcement proceedings

It shall be an unlawful employment practice for an employer to discriminate against any of his employees or applicants for employment, for an employment agency, *or joint labor-management committee controlling apprenticeship or other training or retraining, including on-the-job training programs,* to discriminate against any individual, or for a labor organization to discriminate against any member thereof or applicant for membership, because he has opposed any practice made an unlawful employment practice by this subtitle, or because he has made a charge, testified, assisted, or participated in any manner in an investigation, proceeding, or hearing under this subchapter.

(b) Printing or publication of notices or advertisements indicating prohibited preference, limitation, specification, or discrimination; occupational qualification exception

It shall be an unlawful employment practice for an employer, labor organization, employment agency *or joint labor-management committee controlling apprenticeship or other training or retraining, including on-the-job training programs*, to print or publish or cause to be printed or published any notice or advertisement relating to employment by such an employer or membership in or any classification or referral for employment by such a labor organization, or relating to any classification or referral for employment by such an employment agency, *or relating to admission to, or employment in, any program established to provide apprenticeship or other training by such a joint labor-management committee*, indicating any preference, limitation, specification, or discrimination, based on race, color, religion, sex, or national origin, except that such a notice or advertisement may indicate a preference, limitation, specification, or discrimination based on religion, sex, or national origin when religion, sex, or national origin is a bona fide occupational qualification for employment.

Sec. 705 [42 U.S.C. § 2000e–4]. Equal Employment Opportunity Commission

(a) Creation; composition; political representation; appointment; term; vacancies; Chairman and Vice Chairman; duties of Chairman; appointment of personnel; compensation of personnel

There is hereby created a Commission to be known as the Equal Employment Opportunity Commission, which shall be composed of five members, not more than three of whom shall be members of the same political party. *Members of the Commission shall be appointed by the President by and with the advice and consent of the Senate for a term of five years. Any individual chosen to fill a vacancy shall be appointed only for the unexpired term of the member whom he shall succeed, and all members of the Commission shall continue to serve until their successors are appointed and qualified, except that no such member of the Commission shall continue to serve (1) for more than sixty days when the Congress is in session unless a nomination to fill such vacancy shall have been submitted to the Senate, or (2) after the adjournment sine die of the session of the Senate in which such nomination was submitted.* The President shall designate one member to serve as Chairman of the Commission, and one member to serve as Vice Chairman. The Chairman shall be responsible on behalf of the Commission for the administrative operations of the Commission, and *except as provided in subsection (b) of this section, shall appoint, in accordance with the provisions of title 5, governing appointments in the competitive service, such officers, agents, attorneys,* ***administrative law judges****, and employees as he deems necessary to assist it in the performance of its functions and to fix their compensation in accordance with the provisions of chapter 51 and subchapter III of chapter 53 of title 5 relating to classification and General Schedule pay rates:* Provided, *That assignment, removal, and compensation of administrative law judges shall be in accordance with sections 3105, 3344, 5372, and 7521 of title 5, United States Code.*

(b) General Counsel; appointment; term; duties; representation by attorneys and Attorney General

(1) There shall be a General Counsel of the Commission appointed by the President, by and with the advice and consent of the Senate, for a term of four years. The General Counsel shall have responsibility for the conduct of litigation as provided in sections 2000e–5 and 2000e–6. The General Counsel shall have such other duties as the Commission may prescribe or as may be provided by law and shall concur with the Chairman of the Commission on the appointment and supervision of

regional attorneys. The General Counsel of the Commission on the effective date of this Act shall continue in such position and perform the functions specified in this subsection until a successor is appointed and qualified.

(2) Attorneys appointed under this section may, at the direction of the Commission, appear for and represent the Commission in any case in court, provided that the Attorney General shall conduct all litigation to which the Commission is a party in the Supreme Court pursuant to this subchapter.

(c) Exercise of powers during vacancy; quorum

A vacancy in the Commission shall not impair the right of the remaining members to exercise all the powers of the Commission and three members thereof shall constitute a quorum.

(d) Seal; judicial notice

The Commission shall have an official seal which shall be judicially noticed.

(e) Reports to Congress and the President

The Commission shall at the close of each fiscal year report to the Congress and to the President concerning the action it has taken and the moneys it has disbursed. It shall make such further reports on the cause of and means of eliminating discrimination and such recommendations for further legislation as may appear desirable.

(f) Principal and other offices

The principal office of the Commission shall be in or near the District of Columbia, but it may meet or exercise any or all its powers at any other place. The Commission may establish such regional or State offices as it deems necessary to accomplish the purpose of this subchapter.

(g) Powers of Commission

The Commission shall have power—

(1) to cooperate with and, with their consent, utilize regional, State, local, and other agencies, both public and private, and individuals;

(2) to pay to witnesses whose depositions are taken or who are summoned before the Commission or any of its agents the same witness and mileage fees as are paid to witnesses in the courts of the United States;

(3) to furnish to persons subject to this subchapter such technical assistance as they may request to further their compliance with this subchapter or an order issued thereunder;

(4) upon the request of (i) any employer, whose employees or some of them, or (ii) any labor organization, whose members or some of them,

refuse or threaten to refuse to cooperate in effectuating the provisions of this subchapter, to assist in such effectuation by conciliation or such other remedial action as is provided by this subchapter;

(5) to make such technical studies as are appropriate to effectuate the purposes and policies of this subchapter and to make the results of such studies available to the public;

(6) to *intervene* in a civil action brought *under section 2000e–5 of this title by an aggrieved party against a respondent other than a government, governmental agency or political subdivision.*

(h) Cooperation with other departments and agencies in performance of educational or promotional activities; outreach activities

(1) The Commission shall, in any of its educational or promotional activities, cooperate with other departments and agencies in the performance of such educational and promotional activities.

(2) In exercising its powers under this subchapter, the Commission shall carry out educational and outreach activities (including dissemination of information in languages other than English) targeted to—

(A) individuals who historically have been victims of employment discrimination and have not been equitably served by the Commission; and

(B) individuals on whose behalf the Commission has authority to enforce any other law prohibiting employment discrimination, concerning rights and obligations under this subchapter or such law, as the case may be.

(i) Personnel subject to political activity restrictions

All officers, agents, attorneys, and employees of the Commission shall be subject to the provisions of section 7324 of title 5, notwithstanding any exemption contained in such section.

(j) Technical Assistance Training Institute

(1) The Commission shall establish a Technical Assistance Training Institute, through which the Commission shall provide technical assistance and training regarding the laws and regulations enforced by the Commission.

(2) An employer or other entity covered under this subchapter shall not be excused from compliance with the requirements of this subchapter because of any failure to receive technical assistance under this subchapter.

(3) There are authorized to be appropriated to carry out this subsection such sums as may be necessary for fiscal year 1992.

Sec. 706 [42 U.S.C. § 2000e–5]. Enforcement provisions

(a) Power of Commission to prevent unlawful employment practices

The Commission is empowered, as hereinafter provided, to prevent any person from engaging in any unlawful employment practice as set forth in section 703 or 704 of this title.

(b) Charges by persons aggrieved or member of Commission of unlawful employment practices by employers, etc.; filing; allegations; notice to respondent; contents of notice; investigation by Commission; contents of charges; prohibition on disclosure of charges; determination of reasonable cause; conference, conciliation, and persuasion for elimination of unlawful practices; prohibition on disclosure of informal endeavors to end unlawful practices; use of evidence in subsequent proceedings; penalties for disclosure of information; time for determination of reasonable cause

Whenever a charge is filed *by or on behalf of a* person claiming to be aggrieved, or by a member of the Commission, *alleging* that an employer, employment agency, labor organization, *or joint labor-management committee controlling apprenticeship or other training or retraining, including on-the-job training programs,* has engaged in an unlawful employment practice, the Commission shall *serve a notice of the charge (including the date, place and circumstances of the alleged unlawful employment practice) on* such employer, employment agency, labor organization, *or joint labor-management committee* (hereinafter referred to as the "respondent") *within ten days, and shall make an investigation thereof. Charges shall be in writing under oath or affirmation and shall contain such information and be in such form as the Commission requires. Charges* shall not be made public by the Commission. If the Commission *determines* after such investigation that there is *not* reasonable cause to believe that the charge is *true, it shall dismiss the charge and promptly notify the person claiming to be aggrieved and the respondent of its action. In determining whether reasonable cause exists, the Commission shall accord substantial weight to final findings and orders made by State or local authorities in proceedings commenced under State or local law pursuant to the requirements of subsections (c) and (d) of this section. If the Commission determines after such investigation that there is reasonable cause to believe that the charge is true,* the Commission shall endeavor to eliminate any such alleged unlawful employment practice by informal methods of conference, conciliation, and persuasion. Nothing said or done during and as a part of such *informal* endeavors may be made public by the *Commission, its officers or employees, or used as evidence in a subsequent proceeding* without the written consent of the *persons concerned.* Any *person* who *makes* public information in violation of this subsection shall be fined not more than $1,000 or imprisoned *for* not more than one year, or *both. The Commission shall make its determination on reasonable cause as promptly as possible and, so far as practicable, not later than one hundred and twenty days from the filing of the charge or, where applicable under subsection (c) or (d) of this section, from the date upon which the Commission is authorized to take action with respect to the charge.*

(c) State or local enforcement proceedings; notification of State or local authority; time for filing charges with Commission; commencement of proceedings

In the case of an alleged unlawful employment practice occurring in a State, or political subdivision of a State, which has a State or local law prohibiting the unlawful employment practice alleged and establishing or authorizing a State or local authority to grant or seek relief from such practice or to institute criminal proceedings with respect thereto upon receiving notice thereof, no charge may be filed under subsection (b) of this section by the person aggrieved before the expiration of sixty days after proceedings have been commenced under the State or local law, unless such proceedings have been earlier terminated, provided that such sixty-day period shall be extended to one hundred and twenty days during the first year after the effective date of such State or local law. If any requirement for the commencement of such proceedings is imposed by a State or local authority other than a requirement of the filing of a written and signed statement of the facts upon which the proceeding is based, the proceeding shall be deemed to have been commenced for the purposes of this subsection at the time such statement is sent by registered mail to the appropriate State or local authority.

(d) State or local enforcement proceedings; notification of State or local authority; time for action on charges by Commission

In the case of any charge filed by a member of the Commission alleging an unlawful employment practice occurring in a State or political subdivision of a State which has a State or local law prohibiting the practice alleged and establishing or authorizing a State or local authority to grant or seek relief from such practice or to institute criminal proceedings with respect thereto upon receiving notice thereof, the Commission shall, before taking any action with respect to such charge, notify the appropriate State or local officials and, upon request, afford them a reasonable time, but not less than sixty days (provided that such sixty-day period shall be extended to one hundred and twenty days during the first year after the effective date of such State or local law), unless a shorter period is requested, to act under such State or local law to remedy the practice alleged.

(e) Time for filing charges; time for service of notice of charge on respondent; filing of charge by Commission with State or local agency; seniority system[3]

(1) A charge under *this section* shall be filed within *one hundred and eighty* days after the alleged unlawful employment practice occurred *and notice of the charge (including the date, place and circumstances of the alleged unlawful employment practice) shall be served upon the person against whom such charge is made within ten days thereafter,* except that in a case of an unlawful employment practice with respect to which the person aggrieved has *initially instituted proceedings with a State or local agency with authority to grant or seek relief from such practice or to institute criminal proceedings with respect thereto upon receiving notice thereof,* such charge shall be filed by *or on behalf of* the person aggrieved within *three hundred* days after the alleged unlawful employment practice occurred, or within thirty days after receiving notice that the State or local agency has terminated the proceedings under the State or local law, whichever is earlier, and a copy of such charge shall be filed by the Commission with the State or local agency.

(2) For purposes of this section, an unlawful employment practice occurs, with respect to a seniority system that has been adopted for an intentionally discriminatory purpose in violation of this subchapter (whether or not that discriminatory purpose is apparent on the face of the seniority provision), when the seniority system is adopted, when an individual becomes subject to the seniority system, or when a person aggrieved is injured by the application of the seniority system or provision of the system.

(3)(A) For purposes of this section, an unlawful employment practice occurs, with respect to discrimination in compensation in violation of this subchapter, when a discriminatory compensation decision or other practice is adopted, when an individual becomes subject to a discriminatory compensation decision or other practice, or when an individual is affected by application of a discriminatory compensation decision or other practice, including each time wages, benefits, or other compensation is paid, resulting in whole or in part from such a decision or other practice.

(B) In addition to any relief authorized by section 1981a of this title, liability may accrue and an aggrieved person may obtain relief as provided in subsection (g)(1), including recovery of back pay for up to two years preceding the filing of the charge,

3. The text in § 706(e)(3), which is printed in boldface italics, was added by § 3 of the Lilly Ledbetter Fair Pay Act of 2009, Pub.L.No. 111–2, 123 Stat. 5 (2009), which also provides in § 5 that the amendments in § 706(e)(3) "shall apply to claims of discrimination in compensation brought under" title I and § 503 of the Americans with Disabilities Act of 1990 and under §§ 501 and 504 of the Rehabilitation Act of 1973.

where the unlawful employment practices that have occurred during the charge filing period are similar or related to unlawful employment practices with regard to discrimination in compensation that occurred outside the time for filing a charge.

(f) Civil action by Commission, Attorney General, or person aggrieved; preconditions; procedure; appointment of attorney; payment of fees, costs, or security; intervention; stay of Federal proceedings; action for appropriate temporary or preliminary relief pending final disposition of charge; jurisdiction and venue of United States courts; designation of judge to hear and determine case; assignment of case for hearing; expedition of case; appointment of master

(1) If within thirty days after a charge is filed with the Commission or within thirty days after expiration of any period of reference under subsection *(c) or (d)* of this section, the Commission has been unable to *secure from the respondent a conciliation agreement acceptable to the Commission,* the Commission *may bring a civil action against any respondent not a government, governmental agency, or political subdivision named in the charge. In the case of a respondent which is a government, governmental agency, or political subdivision, if the Commission has been unable to secure from the respondent a conciliation agreement acceptable to the Commission, the Commission shall take no further action and shall refer the case to the Attorney General who may bring a civil action against such respondent in the appropriate United States district court. The person or persons aggrieved shall have the right to intervene in a civil action brought by the Commission or the Attorney General in a case involving a government, governmental agency, or political subdivision. If a charge filed with the Commission pursuant to subsection (b) of this section, is dismissed by the Commission, or if within one hundred and eighty days from the filing of such charge or the expiration of any period of reference under subsection (c) or (d) of this section, whichever is later, the Commission has not filed a civil action under this section or the Attorney General has not filed a civil action in a case involving a government, governmental agency, or political subdivision, or the Commission has not entered into a conciliation agreement to which the person aggrieved is a party, the Commission, or the Attorney General in a case involving a government, governmental agency, or political subdivision, shall so notify the person aggrieved and within ninety days after the giving of such notice a civil action may* be brought against the respondent named in the charge (A) by the person claiming to be aggrieved or (B) if such charge was filed by a member of the Commission, by any person whom the charge alleges was aggrieved by the alleged unlawful employment practice. Upon application by the complainant and in such circumstances as the court may deem just, the court may appoint an attorney for such complainant and may authorize the commencement of the action without the payment of fees, costs, or

security. Upon timely application, the court may, in its discretion, permit the *Commission, or the Attorney General in a case involving a government, governmental agency, or political subdivision*, to intervene in such civil action *upon certification* that the case is of general public importance. Upon request, the court may, in its discretion, stay further proceedings for not more than sixty days pending the termination of State or local proceedings described in subsection *(c) or (d) of this section or further* efforts of the Commission to obtain voluntary compliance.

(2) Whenever a charge is filed with the Commission and the Commission concludes on the basis of a preliminary investigation that prompt judicial action is necessary to carry out the purposes of this Act, the Commission, or the Attorney General in a case involving a government, governmental agency, or political subdivision, may bring an action for appropriate temporary or preliminary relief pending final disposition of such charge. Any temporary restraining order or other order granting preliminary or temporary relief shall be issued in accordance with rule 65 of the Federal Rules of Civil Procedure. It shall be the duty of a court having jurisdiction over proceedings under this section to assign cases for hearing at the earliest practicable date and to cause such cases to be in every way expedited.

(3) Each United States district court and each United States court of a place subject to the jurisdiction of the United States shall have jurisdiction of actions brought under this subchapter. Such an action may be brought in any judicial district in the State in which the unlawful employment practice is alleged to have been committed, in the judicial district in which the employment records relevant to such practice are maintained and administered, or in the judicial district in which the aggrieved person would have worked but for the alleged unlawful employment practice, but if the respondent is not found within any such district, such an action may be brought within the judicial district in which the respondent has his principal office. For purposes of sections 1404 and 1406 of title 28, the judicial district in which the respondent has his principal office shall in all cases be considered a district in which the action might have been brought.

(4) It shall be the duty of the chief judge of the district (or in his absence, the acting chief judge) in which the case is pending immediately to designate a judge in such district to hear and determine the case. In the event that no judge in the district is available to hear and determine the case, the chief judge of the district, or the acting chief judge, as the case may be, shall certify this fact to the chief judge of the circuit (or in his absence, the acting chief judge) who shall then designate a district or circuit judge of the circuit to hear and determine the case.

(5) It shall be the duty of the judge designated pursuant to this subsection to assign the case for hearing at the earliest practicable date and to cause the case to be in every way expedited. If such judge has not scheduled the case for trial within one hundred and twenty days after

issue has been joined, that judge may appoint a master pursuant to rule 53 of the Federal Rules of Civil Procedure.

(g) Injunctions; appropriate affirmative action; equitable relief; accrual of back pay; reduction of back pay; limitations on judicial orders

(1) If the court finds that the respondent has intentionally engaged in or is intentionally engaging in an unlawful employment practice charged in the complaint, the court may enjoin the respondent from engaging in such unlawful employment practice, and order such affirmative action as may be appropriate, which may include, *but is not limited to,* reinstatement or hiring of employees, with or without back pay (payable by the employer, employment agency, or labor organization, as the case may be, responsible for the unlawful employment practice), *or any other equitable relief as the court deems appropriate. Back pay liability shall not accrue from a date more than two years prior to the filing of a charge with the Commission.* Interim earnings or amounts earnable with reasonable diligence by the person or persons discriminated against shall operate to reduce the back pay otherwise allowable.

(2)(A) No order of the court shall require the admission or reinstatement of an individual as a member of a union, or the hiring, reinstatement, or promotion of an individual as an employee, or the payment to him of any back pay, if such individual was refused admission, suspended, or expelled, or was refused employment or advancement or was suspended or discharged for any reason other than discrimination on account of race, color, religion, sex, or national origin or in violation of section 2000e–3(a) of this title.

(B) On a claim in which an individual proves a violation under section 2000e–2(m) of this title and a respondent demonstrates that the respondent would have taken the same action in the absence of the impermissible motivating factor, the court—

(i) may grant declaratory relief, injunctive relief (except as provided in clause (ii)), and attorney's fees and costs demonstrated to be directly attributable only to the pursuit of a claim under section 2000e–2(m) of this title; and

(ii) shall not award damages or issue an order requiring any admission, reinstatement, hiring, promotion, or payment, described in subparagraph (A).

(h) Provisions of chapter 6 of title 29 not applicable to civil actions for prevention of unlawful practices

The provisions of chapter 6 of title 29 shall not apply with respect to civil actions brought under this section.

(i) Proceedings by Commission to compel compliance with judicial orders

In any case in which an employer, employment agency, or labor organization fails to comply with an order of a court issued in a civil action brought under *this section,* the Commission may commence proceedings to compel compliance with such order.

(j) Appeals

Any civil action brought under *this section* and any proceedings brought under subsection (i) of this title shall be subject to appeal as provided in sections 1291 and 1292, title 28.

(k) Attorney's fee; liability of Commission and United States for costs

In any action or proceeding under this subchapter the court, in its discretion, may allow the prevailing party, other than the Commission or the United States, a reasonable attorney's fee **(including expert fees)** as part of the costs, and the Commission and the United States shall be liable for costs the same as a private person.

Sec. 707 [42 U.S.C. § 2000e–6]. Civil actions by the Attorney General

(a) Complaint

Whenever the Attorney General has reasonable cause to believe that any person or group of persons is engaged in a pattern or practice of resistance to the full enjoyment of any of the rights secured by this subchapter, and that the pattern or practice is of such a nature and is intended to deny the full exercise of the rights herein described, the Attorney General may bring a civil action in the appropriate district court of the United States by filing with it a complaint (1) signed by him (or in his absence the Acting Attorney General), (2) setting forth facts pertaining to such pattern or practice, and (3) requesting such relief, including an application for a permanent or temporary injunction, restraining order or other order against the person or persons responsible for such pattern or practice, as he deems necessary to insure the full enjoyment of the rights herein described.

(b) Jurisdiction; three-judge district court for cases of general public importance: hearing, determination, expedition of action, review by Supreme Court; single judge district court: hearing, determination, expedition of action

The district courts of the United States shall have and shall exercise jurisdiction of proceedings instituted pursuant to this section, and in any such proceeding the Attorney General may file with the clerk of such court a request that a court of three judges be convened to hear and determine the case. Such request by the Attorney General shall be accompanied by a certificate that, in his opinion, the case is of general public importance. A copy of the certificate and request for a three-judge court shall be immediately furnished by such clerk to the chief judge of the circuit (or in his absence, the presiding circuit judge of the circuit) in which the case is pending. Upon receipt of such request it shall be the duty of the chief judge of the circuit or the presiding circuit judge, as the case may be, to designate immediately three judges in such circuit, of whom at least one shall be a circuit judge and another of whom shall be a district judge of the court in which the proceeding was instituted, to hear and determine such case, and it shall be the duty of the judges so designated to assign the case for hearing at the earliest practicable date, to participate in the hearing and determination thereof, and to cause the case to be in every way expedited. An appeal from the final judgment of such court will lie to the Supreme Court.

In the event the Attorney General fails to file such a request in any such proceeding, it shall be the duty of the chief judge of the district (or in his absence, the acting chief judge) in which the case is pending immediately to designate a judge in such district to hear and determine the case. In the event that no judge in the district is available to hear and determine the case, the chief judge of the district, or the acting chief judge, as the case may be, shall certify this fact to the chief judge of the circuit (or in his absence, the acting chief judge) who shall then designate a district or circuit judge of the circuit to hear and determine the case.

It shall be the duty of the judge designated pursuant to this section to assign the case for hearing at the earliest practicable date and to cause the case to be in every way expedited.

(c) Transfer of functions, etc., to Commission; effective date; prerequisite to transfer; execution of functions by Commission

Effective two years after March 24, 1972, the functions of the Attorney General under this section shall be transferred to the Commission, together with such personnel, property, records, and unexpended balances of appropriations, allocations, and other funds employed, used, held, available, or to be made available in connection with such functions unless the President submits, and neither House of Congress vetoes, a reorganization plan pursuant to chapter 9 of title 5, inconsistent with the provisions of this subsection. The Commission shall carry out such functions in accordance with subsections (d) and (e) of this section.

(d) Transfer of functions, etc., not to affect suits commenced pursuant to this section prior to date of transfer

Upon the transfer of functions provided for in subsection (c) of this section, in all suits commenced pursuant to this section prior to the date of such transfer, proceedings shall continue without abatement, all court orders and decrees shall remain in effect, and the Commission shall be substituted as a party for the United States of America, the Attorney General, or the Acting Attorney General, as appropriate.

(e) Investigation and action by Commission pursuant to filing of charge of discrimination; procedure

Subsequent to March 24, 1972, the Commission shall have authority to investigate and act on a charge of a pattern or practice of discrimina-

tion, whether filed by or on behalf of a person claiming to be aggrieved or by a member of the Commission. All such actions shall be conducted in accordance with the procedures set forth in section 2000e–5 of this title.

Sec. 708 [42 U.S.C. § 2000e–7]. Effect on State laws

Nothing in this subchapter shall be deemed to exempt or relieve any person from any liability, duty, penalty, or punishment provided by any present or future law of any State or political subdivision of a State, other than any such law which purports to require or permit the doing of any act which would be an unlawful employment practice under this subchapter.

Sec. 709 [42 U.S.C. § 2000e–8]. Investigations

(a) Examination and copying of evidence related to unlawful employment practices

In connection with any investigation of a charge filed under section 2000e–5 of this title, the Commission or its designated representative shall at all reasonable times have access to, for the purposes of examination, and the right to copy any evidence of any person being investigated or proceeded against that relates to unlawful employment practices covered by this subchapter and is relevant to the charge under investigation.

(b) Cooperation with State and local agencies administering State fair employment practices laws; participation in and contribution to research and other projects; utilization of services; payment in advance or reimbursement; agreements and rescission of agreements

The Commission may cooperate with State and local agencies charged with the administration of State fair employment practices laws and, with the consent of such agencies, may, for the purpose of carrying out its functions and duties under this subchapter and within the limitation of funds appropriated specifically for such purpose, *engage in and contribute to the cost of research and other projects of mutual interest undertaken by such agencies, and* utilize the services of such agencies and their employees, and, notwithstanding any other provision of law, *pay by advance or reimbursement* such agencies and their employees for services rendered to assist the Commission in carrying out this subchapter. In furtherance of such cooperative efforts, the Commission may enter into written agreements with such State or local agencies and such agreements may include provisions under which the Commission shall refrain from processing a charge in any cases or class of cases specified in such agreements or under which the Commission shall relieve any person or class of persons in such State or locality from requirements imposed under this section. The Commission shall rescind any such agreement whenever it determines that the agreement no longer serves the interest of effective enforcement of this subchapter.

(c) Execution, retention, and preservation of records; reports to Commission; training program records; appropriate relief from regulation or order for undue hardship; procedure for exemption; judicial action to compel compliance

Every employer, employment agency, and labor organization subject to this subchapter shall (1) make and keep such records relevant to the determinations of whether unlawful employment practices have been or are being committed, (2) preserve such records for such periods, and (3) make such reports therefrom as the Commission shall prescribe by regulation or order, after public hearing, as reasonable, necessary, or appropriate for the enforcement of this subchapter or the regulations or orders thereunder. The Commission shall, by regulation, require each employer, labor organization, and joint labor-management committee subject to this subchapter which controls an apprenticeship or other training program to maintain such records as are reasonably necessary to carry out the purposes of this subchapter, including, but not limited to, a list of applicants who wish to participate in such program, including the chronological order in which applications were received, and to furnish to the Commission upon request, a detailed description of the manner in which persons are selected to participate in the apprenticeship or other training program. Any employer, employment agency, labor organization, or joint labor-management committee which believes that the application to it of any regulation or order issued under this section would result in undue hardship may apply to the Commission for an exemption from the application of such regulation or order, *and, if such application for an exemption is denied,* bring a civil action in the United States district court for the district where such records are kept. If the Commission or the court, as the case may be, finds that the application of the regulation or order to the employer, employment agency, or labor organization in question would impose an undue hardship, the Commission or the court, as the case may be, may grant appropriate relief. *If any person required to comply with the provisions of this subsection fails or refuses to do so, the United States district court for the district in which such person is found, resides, or transacts business, shall, upon application of the Commission, or the Attorney General in a case involving a government, governmental agency or political subdivision, have jurisdiction to issue to such person an order requiring him to comply.*

(d) Consultation and coordination between Commission and interested State and Federal agencies in prescribing recordkeeping and reporting requirements; availability of information furnished pursuant to recordkeeping and reporting requirements; conditions on availability

In prescribing requirements pursuant to subsection (c) of this section, the Commission shall consult with other interested State and Federal agencies and shall endeavor to coordinate its requirements with those adopted by such agencies. The Commission shall furnish upon request and without cost to any State or local agency, charged with the administration of a fair employment practice law information obtained pursuant to subsection (c) of this section from any employer, employment agency, labor organization, or joint labor-management committee subject to the jurisdiction of such agency. Such information shall be furnished on condition that it not be made public by the recipient agency prior to the institution of a proceeding under State or local law involving such information. If this condition is violated by a recipient agency, the Commission may decline to honor subsequent requests pursuant to this subsection.

(e) Prohibited disclosures; penalties

It shall be unlawful for any officer or employee of the Commission to make public in any manner whatever any information obtained by the Commission pursuant to its authority under this section prior to the institution of any proceeding under this subchapter involving such information. Any officer or employee of the Commission who shall make public in any manner whatever any information in violation of this subsection shall be guilty, of a misdemeanor and upon conviction thereof, shall be fined not more than $1,000, or imprisoned not more than one year.

Sec. 710 [42 U.S.C. § 2000e–9]. Conduct of hearings and investigations pursuant to section 161 of title 29

For the purpose of all hearings and investigations conducted by the Commission or its duly authorized agents or agencies, section 161 of title 29 [National Labor Relations Act] shall apply.

Sec. 711 [42 U.S.C. § 2000e–10]. Posting of notices; penalties

(a) Every employer, employment agency, and labor organization, as the case may be, shall post and keep posted in conspicuous places upon its premises where notices to employees, applicants for employment, and members are customarily posted a notice to be prepared or approved by the Commission setting forth excerpts from, or summaries of, the pertinent provisions of this subchapter and information pertinent to the filing of a complaint.

(b) A willful violation of this section shall be punishable by a fine of not more than $100 for each separate offense.

Sec. 712 [42 U.S.C. § 2000e–11]. Veterans' special rights or preferences

Nothing contained in this subchapter shall be construed to repeal or modify any Federal, State, territorial, or local law creating special rights or preference for veterans.

Sec. 713 [42 U.S.C. § 2000e–12]. Regulations; conformity of regulations with administrative procedure provisions; reliance on interpretations and instructions of Commission

(a) The Commission shall have authority from time to time to issue, amend, or rescind suitable procedural regulations to carry out the provisions of this subchapter. Regulations issued under this section shall be in conformity with the standards and limitations of subchapter II of chapter 5 of title 5.

(b) In any action or proceeding based on any alleged unlawful employment practice, no person shall be subject to any liability or punishment for or on account of (1) the commission by such person of an unlawful employment practice if he pleads and proves that the act or omission complained of was in good faith, in conformity with, and in reliance on any written interpretation or opinion of the Commission, or (2) the failure of such person to publish and file any information required by any provision of this subchapter if he pleads and proves that he failed to publish and file such information in good faith, in conformity with the instructions of the Commission issued under this subchapter regarding the filing of such information. Such a defense, if established, shall be a bar to the action or proceeding, notwithstanding that (A) after such act or omission, such interpretation or opinion is modified or rescinded or is determined by judicial authority to be invalid or of no legal effect, or (B) after publishing or filing the description and annual reports, such publication or filing is determined by judicial authority not to be in conformity with the requirements of this subchapter.

Sec. 714 [42 U.S.C. § 2000e–13]. Application to personnel of Commission of sections 111 and 1114 of title 18; punishment of violation of section 1114 of title 18

The provisions of *sections 111 and 1114*, title 18, shall apply to officers, agents, and employees of the Commission in the performance of their official duties. *Notwithstanding the provisions of section 111 and 1114 of title 18, whoever in violation of the provisions of section 1114 of such title kills a person while engaged in or on account of the performance of his official functions under this Act shall be punished by imprisonment for any term of years or for life.*

Sec. 715 [42 U.S.C. § 2000e–14]. Equal Employment Opportunity Coordinating Council; establishment; composition; duties; report to President and Congress

The Equal Employment Opportunity Council shall have the responsibility for developing and implementing agreements, policies and practices designed to maximize effort, promote efficiency, and eliminate conflict, competition, duplication and inconsistency among the operations, functions and jurisdictions of the various departments, agencies and branches of the Federal Government responsible for the implementation and enforcement of equal employment opportunity legislation, orders, and policies. On or before October 1 of each year, the Equal Employment Opportunity Council shall transmit to the President and to the Congress a report of its activities, together with such recommendations for legislative or administrative changes as it concludes are desirable to further promote the purposes of this section.[4]

Sec. 716 [42 U.S.C. § 2000e–15]. Presidential conferences; acquaintance of leadership with provisions for employment rights and obligations; plans for fair administration; membership

The President shall, as soon as feasible after July 2, 1964, convene one or more conferences for the purpose of enabling the leaders of groups whose members will be affected by this subchapter to become familiar with the rights afforded and obligations imposed by its provisions, and for the purpose of making plans which will result in the fair and effective administration of this subchapter when all of its provisions become effective. The President shall invite the participation in such conference or conferences of (1) the members of the President's Committee on Equal Employment Opportunity, (2) the member of the Commission on Civil Rights, (3) representatives of State and local agencies engaged in furthering equal employment opportunity, (4) representatives of private agencies engaged in furthering equal employment opportunity, and (5) representatives of employers, labor organizations, and employment agencies who will be subject to this subchapter.

Sec. 717 [42 U.S.C. 2000e–16]. Employment by Federal Government

(a) Discriminatory practices prohibited; employees or applicants for employment subject to coverage

All personnel actions affecting employees or applicants for employment (except with regard to aliens employed outside the limits of the United States) in military departments as defined in section 102 of title 5, in executive agencies as defined in section 105 of title 5 (including employees and applicants for employment who are paid from nonappropriated funds), in the United States Postal Service and the Postal Rate Commission, in those units of the Government of the District of Columbia having positions in the competitive service, and in those units of the legislative and judicial branches of the Federal Government having positions in the competitive service, and in the Library of Congress shall be made free from any discrimination based on race, color, religion, sex, or national origin.

4. As amended by Reorganization Plan No. 1 of 1978, 43 Fed.Reg. 19807 and Executive Order 12067, 43 Fed.Reg. 28967 (June 30, 1978).

(b) Equal Employment Opportunity Commission; enforcement powers, issuance of rules, regulations, etc.; annual review and approval of national and regional equal employment opportunity plans; review and evaluation of equal employment opportunity programs and publication of progress reports; consultations with interested parties; compliance with rules, regulations, etc.; contents of national and regional equal employment opportunity plans; authority of Librarian of Congress

Except as otherwise provided in this subsection, the Equal Employment Opportunity Commission shall have authority to enforce the provisions of subsection (a) of this section through appropriate remedies, including reinstatement or hiring of employees with or without back pay, as will effectuate the policies of this section, and shall issue such rules, regulations, orders, and instructions as it deems necessary and appropriate to carry out its responsibilities under this section. The Equal Employment Opportunity Commission shall—

(1) be responsible for the annual review and approval of a national and regional equal employment opportunity plan which each department and agency and each appropriate unit referred to in subsection (a) of this section shall submit in order to maintain an affirmative program of equal employment opportunity for all such employees and applicants for employment;

(2) be responsible for the review and evaluation of the operation of all agency equal employment opportunity programs, periodically obtaining and publishing (on at least a semiannual basis) progress reports from each such department, agency, or unit; and

(3) consult with and solicit the recommendations of interested individuals, groups, and organizations relating to equal employment opportunity.

The head of each such department, agency, or unit shall comply with such rules, regulations, orders, and instructions which shall include a provision that an employee or applicant for employment shall be notified of any final action taken on any complaint of discrimination filed by him thereunder. The plan submitted by each department, agency, and unit shall include, but not be limited to—

(1) provision for the establishment of training and education programs designed to provide a maximum opportunity for employees to advance so as to perform at their highest potential; and

(2) a description of the qualifications in terms of training and experience relating to equal employment opportunity for the principal and operating officials of each such department, agency, or unit responsible for carrying out the equal employment opportunity program and of the allocation of personnel and resources proposed by such department, agency, or unit to carry out its equal employment opportunity program.

With respect to employment in the Library of Congress, authorities granted in this subsection to the Equal Employment Opportunity Commission shall be exercised by the Librarian of Congress.

(c) Civil action by employee or applicant for employment for redress of grievances; time for bringing of action; head of department, agency, or unit as defendant

Within 90 days of receipt of notice of final action taken by a department, agency, or unit referred to in subsection (a) of this section, or by the Equal Employment Opportunity Commission upon an appeal from a decision or order of such department, agency, or unit on a complaint of discrimination based on race, color, religion, sex, or national origin, brought pursuant to subsection (a) of this section, Executive Order 11478 or any succeeding Executive orders, or after one hundred and eighty days from the filing of the initial charge with the department, agency, or unit or with the Equal Employment Opportunity Commission on appeal from a decision or order of such department, agency, or unit until such time as final action may be taken by a department, agency, or unit, an employee or applicant for employment, if aggrieved by the final disposition of his complaint, or by the failure to take final action on his complaint, may file a civil action as provided in section 2000e–5 of this title, in which civil action the head of the department, agency, or unit, as appropriate, shall be the defendant.

(d) Section 2000e–5(f) through (k) of this title applicable to civil actions

The provisions of section 2000e–5(f) through (k) of this title, as applicable, shall govern civil actions brought hereunder, **and the same interest to compensate for delay in payment shall be available as in cases involving nonpublic parties.**

(e) Government agency or official not relieved of responsibility to assure nondiscrimination in employment or equal employment opportunity

Nothing contained in this Act shall relieve any Government agency or official of its or his primary responsibility to assure nondiscrimination in employment as required by the Constitution and statutes or of its or his responsibilities under Executive Order 11478 relating to equal employment opportunity in the Federal Government.

(f) Section 706(e)(3) shall apply to complaints of discrimination in compensation under this section.

Sec. 718 [42 U.S.C. § 2000e–17]. Procedure for denial, withholding, termination, or suspension of Government contract subsequent to acceptance by Government of affirmative action plan of employer; time of acceptance of plan

No Government contract, or portion thereof, with any employer, shall be denied, withheld, terminated, or suspended, by any agency or officer of the United States under any equal employment opportunity law or order, where such employer has an affirmative action plan which has previously been accepted by the Government for the same facility within the past twelve months without first according such employer full hearing and adjudication under the provisions of section 554 of title 5, and the following pertinent sections: Provided, That if such employer has deviated substantially from such previously agreed to affirmative action plan, this section shall not apply: Provided further, That for the purposes of this section an affirmative action plan shall be deemed to have been accepted by the Government at the time the appropriate compliance agency has accepted such plan unless within forty-five days thereafter the Office of Federal Contract Compliance has disapproved such plan.

CIVIL RIGHTS ACT OF 1991
Pub.L.No. 102–166, 105 Stat. 1071 (1991)

Sec. 1. Short Title

This Act may be cited as the "Civil Rights Act of 1991".

Sec. 2. Findings

The Congress finds that—

(1) additional remedies under Federal law are needed to deter unlawful harassment and intentional discrimination in the workplace;

(2) the decision of the Supreme Court in *Wards Cove Packing Co. v. Atonio*, 490 U.S. 642 (1989), has weakened the scope and effectiveness of Federal civil rights protections; and

(3) legislation is necessary to provide additional protections against unlawful discrimination in employment.

Sec. 3. Purposes

The purposes of this Act are—

(1) to provide appropriate remedies for intentional discrimination and unlawful harassment in the workplace;

(2) to codify the concepts of "business necessity" and "job related" enunciated by the Supreme Court in *Griggs v. Duke Power Co.*, 401 U.S. 424 (1971), and in the other Supreme Court decisions prior to *Wards Cove Packing Co. v. Atonio*, 490 U.S. 642 (1989);

(3) to confirm statutory authority and provide statutory guidelines for the adjudication of disparate impact suits under title VII of the Civil Rights Act of 1964 [42 U.S.C. § 2000e et seq.]; and

(4) to respond to recent decisions of the Supreme Court by expanding the scope of relevant civil rights statutes in order to provide adequate protection to victims of discrimination.

TITLE I—FEDERAL CIVIL RIGHTS REMEDIES

* * *

Sec. 116. Lawful Court–Ordered Remedies, Affirmative Action, and Conciliation Agreements Not Affected

Nothing in the amendments made by this title shall be construed to affect court-ordered remedies, affirmative action, or conciliation agreements, that are in accordance with the law.

* * *

Sec. 118. Alternative Means of Dispute Resolution

Where appropriate and to the extent authorized by law, the use of alternative means of dispute resolution, including settlement negotiations, conciliation, facilitation, mediation, factfinding, minitrials, and arbitration, is encouraged to resolve disputes arising under the Acts or provisions of Federal law amended by this title.

LILLY LEDBETTER FAIR PAY ACT OF 2009
Pub.L.No. 111–2, 123 Stat. 5 (2009)

Sec. 1. Short Title

This Act may be cited as the "Lilly Ledbetter Fair Pay Act of 2009".

Sec. 2. Findings

Congress finds the following:

(1) The Supreme Court in *Ledbetter v. Goodyear Tire & Rubber Co.*, 550 U.S. 618 (2007), significantly impairs statutory protections against discrimination in compensation that Congress established and that have been bedrock principles of American law for decades. The Ledbetter decision undermines those statutory protections by unduly restricting the time period in which victims of discrimination can challenge and recover for discriminatory compensation decisions or other practices, contrary to the intent of Congress.

(2) The limitation imposed by the Court on the filing of discriminatory compensation claims ignores the reality of wage discrimination and is at odds with the robust application of the civil rights laws that Congress intended.

(3) With regard to any charge of discrimination under any law, nothing in this Act is intended to preclude or limit an aggrieved person's right to introduce evidence of an unlawful employment practice that has occurred outside the time for filing a charge of discrimination.

(4) Nothing in this Act is intended to change current law treatment of when pension distributions are considered paid.

* * *

Sec. 6. Effective Date

This Act, and the amendments made by this Act, take effect as if enacted on May 28, 2007 and apply to all claims of discrimination in compensation under title VII of the Civil Rights Act of 1964 (42 U.S.C. 2000e et seq.), the Age Discrimination in Employment Act of 1967 (29 U.S.C. 621 et seq.), title I and section 503 of the Americans with Disabilities Act of 1990, and sections 501 and 504 of the Rehabilitation Act of 1973, that are pending on or after that date.

AGE DISCRIMINATION IN EMPLOYMENT ACT OF 1967
29 U.S.C. §§ 621–634

Sec. 2 [29 U.S.C. § 621]. Congressional statement of findings and purpose[1]

(a) The Congress hereby finds and declares that—

(1) in the face of rising productivity and affluence, older workers find themselves disadvantaged in their efforts to retain employment, and especially to regain employment when displaced from jobs;

(2) the setting of arbitrary age limits regardless of potential for job performance has become a common practice, and certain otherwise desirable practices may work to the disadvantage of older persons;

(3) the incidence of unemployment, especially long-term unemployment with resultant deterioration of skill, morale, and employer acceptability is, relative to the younger ages, high among older workers; their numbers are great and growing; and their employment problems grave;

(4) the existence in industries affecting commerce, of arbitrary discrimination in employment because of age, burdens commerce and the free flow of goods in commerce.

(b) It is therefore the purpose of this chapter to promote employment of older persons based on their ability rather than age; to prohibit arbitrary age discrimination in employment; to help employers and workers find ways of meeting problems arising from the impact of age on employment.

Sec. 3 [29 U.S.C. § 622]. Education and research program; recommendation to Congress

(a) The Secretary of Labor[2] shall undertake studies and provide information to labor unions, management, and the general public con-

1. Section 101 of the Older Worker Benefit Protection Act, Pub.L.No. 101–433, 104 Stat. 978 (1990), codified as a Note to § 621, states:

> The Congress finds that, as a result of the decision of the Supreme Court in *Public Employees Retirement System of Ohio v. Betts*, 109 S.Ct. 256 (1989), legislative action is necessary to restore the original congressional intent in passing and amending the Age Discrimination in Employment Act of 1967 [29 U.S.C. 621 et seq.], which was to prohibit discrimination against older workers in all employee benefits except when age-based reductions in employee benefit plans are justified by significant cost considerations.

2. Transfer of Functions. The "Equal Employment Opportunity Commission"

cerning the needs and abilities of older workers, and their potentials for continued employment and contribution to the economy. In order to achieve the purposes of this chapter, the Secretary of Labor shall carry on a continuing program of education and information, under which he may, among other measures—

(1) undertake research, and promote research, with a view to reducing barriers to the employment of older persons, and the promotion of measures for utilizing their skills;

(2) publish and otherwise make available to employers, professional societies, the various media of communication, and other interested persons the findings of studies and other materials for the promotion of employment;

(3) foster through the public employment service system and through cooperative effort the development of facilities of public and private agencies for expanding the opportunities and potentials of older persons;

(4) sponsor and assist State and community informational and educational programs.

(b) Not later than six months after the effective date of this chapter, the Secretary shall recommend to the Congress any measures he may deem desirable to change the lower or upper age limits set forth in section 631 of this title.

Sec. 4 [29 U.S.C. § 623]. Prohibition of age discrimination

(a) Employer practices

It shall be unlawful for an employer—

(1) to fail or refuse to hire or to discharge any individual or otherwise discriminate against any individual with respect to his compensation, terms, conditions, or privileges of employment, because of such individual's age;

(2) to limit, segregate, or classify his employees in any way which would deprive or tend to deprive any individual of employment opportunities or otherwise adversely affect his status as an employee, because of such individual's age; or

(3) to reduce the wage rate of any employee in order to comply with this chapter.

(b) Employment agency practices

It shall be unlawful for an employment agency to fail or refuse to refer for employment, or otherwise to discriminate against, any individu-

and "Commission" were substituted for "Secretary," meaning the Secretary of Labor, pursuant to Reorganization Plan No. 1 of 1978, § 2, 43 Fed.Reg. 19807, 92 Stat. 3781, set out in Appendix 1 to title 5, Government Reorganization and Employees, which transferred all functions vested by this section in the Secretary of Labor to the Equal Employment Opportunity Commission, effective Jan. 1, 1979, as provided by section 1–101 of Executive Order No. 12106, Dec. 28, 1978, 44 Fed.Reg. 1053.

al because of such individual's age, or to classify or refer for employment any individual on the basis of such individual's age.

(c) Labor organization practices

It shall be unlawful for a labor organization—

(1) to exclude or to expel from its membership, or otherwise to discriminate against, any individual because of his age;

(2) to limit, segregate, or classify its membership, or to classify or fail or refuse to refer for employment any individual, in any way which would deprive or tend to deprive any individual of employment opportunities, or would limit such employment opportunities or otherwise adversely affect his status as an employee or as an applicant for employment, because of such individual's age;

(3) to cause or attempt to cause an employer to discriminate against an individual in violation of this section.

(d) Opposition to unlawful practices; participation in investigations, proceedings, or litigation

It shall be unlawful for an employer to discriminate against any of his employees or applicants for employment, for an employment agency to discriminate against any individual, or for a labor organization to discriminate against any member thereof or applicant for membership, because such individual, member or applicant for membership has opposed any practice made unlawful by this section, or because such individual, member or applicant for membership has made a charge, testified, assisted, or participated in any manner in an investigation, proceeding, or litigation under this chapter.

(e) Printing or publication of notice or advertisement indicating preference, limitation, etc.

It shall be unlawful for an employer, labor organization, or employment agency to print or publish, or cause to be printed or published, any notice or advertisement relating to employment by such an employer or membership in or any classification or referral for employment by such a labor organization, or relating to any classification or referral for employment by such an employment agency, indicating any preference, limitation, specification, or discrimination, based on age.

(f) Lawful practices; age and occupational qualification; other reasonable factors; laws of foreign workplace; seniority system; employee benefit plans; discharge or discipline for good cause

It shall not be unlawful for any employer, employment agency, or labor organization—

(1) to take any action otherwise prohibited under subsections (a), (b), (c), or (e) of this section where age is a bona fide occupational qualification reasonably necessary to the normal operation of the

particular business, or where the differentiation is based on reasonable factors other than age, or where such practices involve an employee in a workplace in a foreign country, and compliance with such subsections would cause such employer, or a corporation controlled by such employer, to violate the laws of the country in which such workplace is located;

(2) to take any action otherwise prohibited under subsection (a), (b), (c), or (e) of this section—

(A) to observe the terms of a bona fide seniority system that is not intended to evade the purposes of this chapter, except that no such seniority system shall require or permit the involuntary retirement of any individual specified by section 631(a) of this title because of the age of such individual; or

(B) to observe the terms of a bona fide employee benefit plan—

(i) where, for each benefit or benefit package, the actual amount of payment made or cost incurred on behalf of an older worker is no less than that made or incurred on behalf of a younger worker, as permissible under section 1625.10, title 29, Code of Federal Regulations (as in effect on June 22, 1989); or

(ii) that is a voluntary early retirement incentive plan consistent with the relevant purpose or purposes of this chapter.

Notwithstanding clause (i) or (ii) of subparagraph (B), no such employee benefit plan or voluntary early retirement incentive plan shall excuse the failure to hire any individual, and no such employee benefit plan shall require or permit the involuntary retirement of any individual specified by section 631(a) of this title, because of the age of such individual. An employer, employment agency, or labor organization acting under subparagraph (A), or under clause (i) or (ii) of subparagraph (B), shall have the burden of proving that such actions are lawful in any civil enforcement proceeding brought under this chapter; or

(3) to discharge or otherwise discipline an individual for good cause.

(g) Repealed

(h) Practices of foreign corporations controlled by American employers; foreign employers not controlled by American employers; factors determining control

(1) If an employer controls a corporation whose place of incorporation is in a foreign country, any practice by such corporation prohibited under this section shall be presumed to be such practice by such employer.

(2) The prohibitions of this section shall not apply where the employer is a foreign person not controlled by an American employer.

(3) For the purpose of this subsection the determination of whether an employer controls a corporation shall be based upon the—

(A) interrelation of operations,

(B) common management,

(C) centralized control of labor relations, and

(D) common ownership or financial control, of the employer and the corporation.

(i) Employee pension benefit plans; cessation or reduction of benefit accrual or of allocation to employee account; distribution of benefits after attainment of normal retirement age; compliance; highly compensated employees

(1) Except as otherwise provided in this subsection, it shall be unlawful for an employer, an employment agency, a labor organization, or any combination thereof to establish or maintain an employee pension benefit plan which requires or permits—

(A) in the case of a defined benefit plan, the cessation of an employee's benefit accrual, or the reduction of the rate of an employee's benefit accrual, because of age, or

(B) in the case of a defined contribution plan, the cessation of allocations to an employee's account or, the reduction of the rate at which amounts are allocated to an employee's account, because of age.

(2) Nothing in this section shall be construed to prohibit an employer, employment agency, or labor organization from observing any provision of an employee pension benefit plan to the extent that such provision imposes (without regard to age) a limitation on the amount of benefits that the plan provides or a limitation on the number of years of service or years of participation which are taken into account for purposes of determining benefit accrual under the plan.

(3) In the case of any employee who, as of the end of any plan year under a defined benefit plan, has attained normal retirement age under such plan—

(A) if distribution of benefits under such plan with respect to such employee has commenced as of the end of such plan year, then any requirement of this subsection for continued accrual of benefits under such plan with respect to such employee during such plan year shall be treated as satisfied to the extent of the actuarial equivalent of in-service distribution of benefits, and

(B) if distribution of benefits under such plan with respect to such employee has not commenced as of the end of such year in accordance with section 1056(a)(3) of this title and section 401(a)(14)(C) of title 26, and the payment of benefits under such plan with respect to such employee is not suspended during such plan year pursuant to section 1053(a)(3)(B) of this title or section 411 (a)(3)(B) of title 26, then any requirement of this subsection for continued accrual of benefits under such plan with respect to such employee during such plan year shall be treated as satisfied to the extent of any adjustment in the benefit payable under the plan during such plan year attributable to the delay in the distribution of benefits after the attainment of normal retirement age.

The provisions of this paragraph shall apply in accordance with regulations of the Secretary of the Treasury. Such regulations shall provide for the application of the preceding provisions of this paragraph to all employee pension benefit plans subject to this subsection and may provide for the application of such provisions, in the case of any such employee, with respect to any period of time within a plan year.

(4) Compliance with the requirements of this subsection with respect to an employee pension benefit plan shall constitute compliance with the requirements of this section relating to benefit accrual under such plan.

(5) Paragraph (1) shall not apply with respect to any employee who is a highly compensated employee (within the meaning of section 414(q) of title 26) to the extent provided in regulations prescribed by the Secretary of Treasury for purposes of precluding discrimination in favor of highly compensated employees within the meaning of subchapter D of chapter 1 of title 26.

(6) A plan shall not be treated as failing to meet the requirements of paragraph (1) solely because the subsidized portion of any early retirement benefit is disregarded in determining benefit accruals **or it is a plan permitted by subsection m.**[3]

(7) Any regulations prescribed by the Secretary of the Treasury pursuant to clause (v) of section 411(b)(1)(H) of title 26 and subparagraphs (C) and (D) of section 411(b)(2) of title 26 shall apply with respect to the requirements of this subsection in the same manner and to the same extent as such regulations apply with respect to the requirements of such sections 411(b)(1)(H) and 411(b)(2) of title 26.

(8) A plan shall not be treated as failing to meet the requirements of this section solely because such plan provides a normal retirement age described in section 1002(24)(B) of this title and section 411(a)(8)(B) of title 26.

(9) For purposes of this subsection—

(A) The terms "employee pension benefit plan," "defined benefit plan," "defined contribution plan," and "normal retirement age" have the meanings provided such terms in section 1002 of this title.

3. The boldface phrase was added by Part D of the Higher Education Amendments of 1998, Pub.L.No. 105–244 (1998).

(B) The term "compensation" has the meaning provided by section 414(s) of title 26.

(j) Employment as firefighter or law enforcement officer.[4]

It shall not be an unlawful for an employer which is a State, a political subdivision of a State, an agency or instrumentality of a State or a political subdivision of a State, or an interstate agency to fail or refuse to hire or to discharge any individual because of such individual's age if such action is taken—

(1) with respect to the employment of an individual as a firefighter or as a law enforcement officer, the employer has complied with section 3(d)(2) of the Age Discrimination in Employment Amendments of 1996 if the individual was discharged after the date described in such section, and the individual has attained—

(A) the age of hiring or retirement, respectively, in effect under applicable State or local law on March 3, 1983; or

(B)(i) if the individual was not hired, the age of hiring in effect on the date of such failure or refusal to hire under applicable State or local law enacted after September 30, 1996; or

(ii) if applicable State or local law was enacted after September 30, 1996, and the individual was discharged, the higher of—

(I) the age of retirement in effect on the date of such discharge under such law; and

(II) age 55; and

(2) pursuant to a bona fide hiring or retirement plan that is not a subterfuge to evade the purposes of this chapter.

(k) Seniority system or employee benefit plan; compliance

A seniority system or employee benefit plan shall comply with this chapter regardless of the date of adoption of such system or plan.

(*l*) Lawful practices; minimum age as a condition of eligibility for retirement benefits; deductions from severance pay; reduction of long-term disability benefits[5]

Notwithstanding clause (i) or (ii) of subsection (f)(2)(B) of this section—

4. The earlier exemption for public firefighters and law enforcement officers expired on December 31, 1993. Congress reinstated the exemption, as amended, in the Age Discrimination in Employment Amendments of 1996. Pub.L.No. 104–208, 110 Stat. 3009 § 119 (1996).

5. As amended by the Older Worker Benefit Protection Act, Technical Amendment, Pub.L.No. 101–521, 104 Stat. 2287 (1990).

(1) It shall not be a violation of subsection (a), (b), (c), or (e) of this section solely because—

(A) an employee pension benefit plan (as defined in section 1002(2) of this title) [Employee Retirement Income Security Act of 1974 (29 U.S.C. § 10002(2))] provides for the attainment of a minimum age as a condition of eligibility for normal or early retirement benefits; or

(B) a defined benefit plan (as defined in section 3(35) of such Act) provides for—

(i) payments that constitute the subsidized portion of an early retirement benefit; or

(ii) social security supplements for plan participants that commence before the age and terminate at the age (specified by the plan) when participants are eligible to receive reduced or unreduced old-age insurance benefits under title II of the Social Security Act (42 U.S.C. § 401 et seq.), and that do not exceed such old-age insurance benefits.

(2)(A) It shall not be a violation of subsection (a), (b), (c), or (e) of this section solely because following a contingent event unrelated to age—

(i) the value of any retiree health benefits received by an individual eligible for an immediate pension;

(ii) the value of any additional pension benefits that are made available solely as a result of the contingent event unrelated to age and following which the individual is eligible for not less than an immediate and unreduced pension; or

(iii) the values described in both clauses (i) and (ii);

are deducted from severance pay made available as a result of the contingent event unrelated to age.

(B) For an individual who receives immediate pension benefits that are actually reduced under subparagraph (A)(i), the amount of the deduction available pursuant to subparagraph (A)(i) shall be reduced by the same percentage as the reduction in the pension benefits.

(C) For purposes of this paragraph, severance pay shall include that portion of supplemental unemployment compensation benefits (as described in section 501(c)(17) of title 26) that—

(i) constitutes additional benefits of up to 52 weeks;

(ii) has the primary purpose and effect of continuing benefits until an individual becomes eligible for an immediate and unreduced pension; and

(iii) is discontinued once the individual becomes eligible for an immediate and unreduced pension.

(D) For purposes of this paragraph and solely in order to make the deduction authorized under this paragraph, the term "retiree health benefits" means benefits provided pursuant to a group health plan covering retirees, for which (determined as of the contingent event unrelated to age)—

(i) the package of benefits provided by the employer for the retirees who are below age 65 is at least comparable to benefits provided under title XVIII of the Social Security Act [42 U.S.C. § 1395 et seq.];

(ii) the package of benefits provided by the employer for the retirees who are age 65 and above is at least comparable to that offered under a plan that provides a benefit package with one-fourth the value of benefits provided under title XVIII of such Act; or

(iii) the package of benefits provided by the employer is as described in clauses (i) and (ii).

(E)(i) If the obligation of the employer to provide retiree health benefits is of limited duration, the value for each individual shall be calculated at a rate of $3,000 per year for benefit years before age 65, and $750 per year for benefit years beginning at age 65 and above.

(ii) If the obligation of the employer to provide retiree health benefits is of unlimited duration, the value for each individual shall be calculated at a rate of $48,000 for individuals below age 65, and $24,000 for individuals age 65 and above.

(iii) The values described in clauses (i) and (ii) shall be calculated based on the age of the individual as of the date of the contingent event unrelated to age. The values are effective on October 16, 1990, and shall be adjusted on an annual basis, with respect to a contingent event that occurs subsequent to the first year after October 16, 1990, based on the medical component of the Consumer Price Index for all-urban consumers published by the Department of Labor.

(iv) If an individual is required to pay a premium for retiree health benefits, the value calculated pursuant to this subparagraph shall be reduced by whatever percentage of the overall premium the individual is required to pay.

(F) If an employer that has implemented a deduction pursuant to subparagraph (A) fails to fulfill the obligation described in subparagraph (E), any aggrieved individual may bring an action for specific performance of the obligation described in subparagraph (E). The relief shall be in addition to any other remedies provided under Federal or State law.

(3) It shall not be a violation of subsection (a), (b), (c), or (e) of this section solely because an employer provides a bona fide employee benefit plan or plans under which long-term disability benefits received by an individual are reduced by any pension benefits (other than those attributable to employee contributions)—

(A) paid to the individual that the individual voluntarily elects to receive; or

(B) for which an individual who has attained the later of age 62 or normal retirement age is eligible.

(m) Voluntary retirement incentive plans.[6]

Notwithstanding subsection (f)(2)(B), it shall not be a violation of subsection (a), (b), (c), or (e) solely because a plan of an institution of higher education (as defined in section 101 of the Higher Education Act of 1965) offers employees who are serving under a contract of unlimited tenure (or similar arrangement providing for unlimited tenure) supplemental benefits upon voluntary retirement that are reduced or eliminated on the basis of age, if—

(1) such institution does not implement with respect to such employees any age-based reduction or cessation of benefits that are not such supplemental benefits, except as permitted by other provisions of this Act;

(2) such supplemental benefits are in addition to any retirement or severance benefits which have been offered generally to employees serving under a contract of unlimited tenure (or similar arrangement providing for unlimited tenure), independent of any early retirement or exit-incentive plan, within the preceding 365 days; and

(3) any employee who attains the minimum age and satisfies all non-age-based conditions for receiving a benefit under the plan has an opportunity lasting not less than 180 days to elect to retire and to receive the maximum benefit that could then be elected by a younger but otherwise similarly situated employee, and the plan does not require retirement to occur sooner than 180 days after such election.

Nothing in [* * * subsection (m)] shall affect the application of section 4 of the Age Discrimination in Employment Act of 1967 [29 U.S.C. § 623] with respect to—

(1) any plan described in subsection (m) of section 4 of such Act for any period prior to enactment of such Act;

(2) any plan not described in subsection (m) of section 4 of such Act; or

(3) any employer other than an institution of higher education (as defined in section 101 of the Higher Education Act of 1965).

Sec. 5 [29 U.S.C. § 624]. Study to analyze potential consequences of elimination of mandatory retirement on institutions of higher education

(1) The Equal Employment Opportunity Commission, shall, not later than 12 months after the date of the enactment of this Act [Oct. 31,

6. Section (m) was added by Part D of the Higher Education Amendments of 1998, Pub.L.No. 105–244 (1998).

1986], enter into an agreement with the National Academy of Sciences for the conduct of a study to analyze the potential consequences of the elimination of mandatory retirement on institutions of higher education.

(2) The study required by paragraph (1) of this subsection shall be conducted under the general supervision of the National Academy of Sciences by a study panel composed of 9 members. The study panel shall consist of—

(A) 4 members who shall be administrators at institutions of higher education selected by the National Academy of Sciences after consultation with the American Council of Education, the Association of American Universities, and the National Association of State Universities and Land Grant Colleges;

(B) 4 members who shall be teachers or retired teachers at institutions of higher education (who do not serve in an administrative capacity at such institutions), selected by the National Academy of Sciences after consultation with the American Federation of Teachers, the National Education Association, the American Association of University Professors, and the American Association of Retired Persons; and

(C) one member selected by the National Academy of Sciences.

(3) The results of the study shall be reported, with recommendations, to the President and to the Congress not later than 5 years after the date of enactment of this Act [Oct. 31, 1986].

(4) The expenses of the study required by this subsection shall be paid from funds available to the Equal Employment Opportunity Commission.

Sec. 6 [29 U.S.C. § 625]. Administration

The Secretary shall have the power—

(a) Delegation of Functions: appointment of personnel; technical assistance

To make delegations, to appoint such agents and employees, and to pay for technical assistance on a fee for service basis, as he deems necessary to assist him in the performance of his functions under this chapter;

(b) Cooperation with other agencies, employers, labor organizations, and employment agencies

To cooperate with regional, State, local, and other agencies, and to cooperate with and furnish technical assistance to employers, labor organizations, and employment agencies to aid in effectuating the purposes of this chapter.

Sec. 7 [29 U.S.C. § 626]. Recordkeeping, investigation, and enforcement

(a) Attendance of witnesses, investigations, inspections, records, and homework regulations

The Equal Employment Opportunity Commission shall have the power to make investigations and require the keeping of records necessary or appropriate for the administration of this chapter in accordance with the powers and procedures provided in sections 209 and 211 of this title.

(b) Enforcement; prohibition of age discrimination under fair labor standards; unpaid minimum wages and unpaid overtime compensation; liquidated damages; judicial relief; conciliation, conference, and persuasion

The provisions of this chapter shall be enforced in accordance with the powers, remedies, and procedures provided in sections 211(b), 216 (except for subsection (a) thereof), and 217 of this title, and subsection (c) of this section. Any act prohibited under section 623 of this title shall be deemed to be a prohibited act under section 215 of this title. Amounts owing to a person as a result of a violation of this chapter shall be deemed to be unpaid minimum wages or unpaid overtime compensation for purposes of sections 216 and 217 of this title: *Provided*, That liquidated damages shall be payable only in cases of willful violations of this chapter. In any action brought to enforce this chapter the court shall have jurisdiction to grant such legal or equitable relief as may be appropriate to effectuate the purposes of this chapter, including without limitation judgments compelling employment, reinstatement or promotion, or enforcing the liability for amounts deemed to be unpaid minimum wages or unpaid overtime compensation under this section. Before instituting any action under this section, the Equal Employment Opportunity Commission shall attempt to eliminate the discriminatory practice or practices alleged, and to effect voluntary compliance with the requirements of this chapter through informal methods of conciliation, conference, and persuasion.

(c) Civil action; persons aggrieved; jurisdiction; judicial relief; termination of individual action upon commencement of action by Commission; jury trial

(1) Any person aggrieved may bring a civil action in any court of competent jurisdiction for such legal or equitable relief as will effectuate the purposes of this chapter: *Provided*, That the right of any person to bring such action shall terminate upon the commencement of an action by the Equal Employment Opportunity Commission to enforce the right of such employee under this chapter.

(2) In an action brought under paragraph (1), a person shall be entitled to a trial by jury of any issue of fact in any such action for recovery of amounts owing as a result of a violation of this chapter,

regardless of whether equitable relief is sought by any party in such action.

(d)(1) No civil action may be commenced by an individual under this section until 60 days after a charge alleging unlawful discrimination has been filed with the Equal Employment Opportunity Commission. Such a charge shall be filed—

(A) within 180 days after the alleged unlawful practice occurred; or

(B) in a case to which section 633(b) of this title applies, within 300 days after the alleged unlawful practice occurred, or within 30 days after receipt by the individual of notice of termination of proceedings under State law, whichever is earlier.

(2) Upon receiving such a charge, the Commission shall promptly notify all persons named in such charge as prospective defendants in the action and shall promptly seek to eliminate any alleged unlawful practice by informal methods of conciliation, conference, and persuasion.

(3) For purposes of this section, an unlawful practice occurs, with respect to discrimination in compensation in violation of this chapter, when a discriminatory compensation decision or other practice is adopted, when a person becomes subject to a discriminatory compensation decision or other practice, or when a person is affected by application of a discriminatory compensation decision or other practice, including each time wages, benefits, or other compensation is paid, resulting in whole or in part from such a decision or other practice.[7]

(e) Reliance on administrative rulings; notice of dismissal or termination; civil action after receipt of notice[8]

Section 259 of this title [Portal-to-Portal Act of 1947] shall apply to actions under this chapter. *If a charge filed with the Commission under this chapter is dismissed or the proceedings of the Commission are otherwise terminated by the Commission, the Commission shall notify the person aggrieved. A civil action may be brought under this section by a person defined in section 630(a) of this title against the respondent named in the charge within 90 days after the date of receipt of such notice.*

(f) Waiver

(1) An individual may not waive any right or claim under this chapter unless the waiver is knowing and voluntary. Except as provided

7. Section 7(d) was amended by § 4 of the Lilly Ledbetter Fair Pay Act of 2009, Pub.L.No. 111–2, 123 Stat. 5 (2009). The 2009 Amendments struck out "(d)" and inserted "(d)(1)"; deleted the heading, "Filing of charge with Commission; timeliness; conciliation, conference, and persuasion"; relabeled paragraphs (1) and (2) as (A) and (B), respectively; numbered the paragraph at the end as paragraph (2); and added a new subsection in paragraph (3), which is printed here in boldface italics.

8. Section 7(e) was amended by the Civil Rights Act of 1991, Pub.L.No. 102–166, 105 Stat. 1071 (1991). The 1991 amendments are printed in italics.

in paragraph (2), a waiver may not be considered knowing and voluntary unless at a minimum—

(A) the waiver is part of an agreement between the individual and the employer that is written in a manner calculated to be understood by such individual, or by the average individual eligible to participate;

(B) the waiver specifically refers to rights or claims arising under this chapter;

(C) the individual does not waive rights or claims that may arise after the date the waiver is executed;

(D) the individual waives rights or claims only in exchange for consideration in addition to anything of value to which the individual already is entitled;

(E) the individual is advised in writing to consult with an attorney prior to executing the agreement;

(F)(i) the individual is given a period of at least 21 days within which to consider the agreement; or

(ii) if a waiver is requested in connection with an exit incentive or other employment termination program offered to a group or class of employees, the individual is given a period of at least 45 days within which to consider the agreement;

(G) the agreement provides that for a period of at least 7 days following the execution of such agreement, the individual may revoke the agreement, and the agreement shall not become effective or enforceable until the revocation period has expired;

(H) if a waiver is requested in connection with an exit incentive or other employment termination program offered to a group or class of employees, the employer (at the commencement of the period specified in subparagraph (F)) informs the individual in writing in a manner calculated to be understood by the average individual eligible to participate, as to—

(i) any class, unit, or group of individuals covered by such program, any eligibility factors of such program, and any time limits applicable to such program; and

(ii) the job titles and ages of all individuals eligible or selected for the program, and the ages of all individuals in the same job classification or organizational unit who are not eligible or selected for the program.

(2) A waiver in settlement of a charge filed with the Equal Employment Opportunity Commission, or an action in court by the individual or the individual's representative, alleging age discrimination of a kind prohibited under section 623 or 633a of this title may not be considered knowing and voluntary unless at a minimum—

(A) subparagraphs (A) through (E) of paragraph (1) have been met; and

(B) the individual is given a reasonable period of time within which to consider the settlement agreement.

(3) In any dispute that may arise over whether any of the requirements, conditions, and circumstances set forth in subparagraph (A), (B), (C), (D), (E), (F), (G), or (H) of paragraph (1), or subparagraph (A) or (B) of paragraph (2), have been met, the party asserting the validity of a waiver shall have the burden of proving in a court of competent jurisdiction that a waiver was knowing and voluntary pursuant to paragraph (1) or (2).

(4) No waiver agreement may affect the Commission's rights and responsibilities to enforce this chapter. No waiver may be used to justify interfering with the protected right of an employee to file a charge or participate in an investigation or proceeding conducted by the Commission.

Sec. 8 [29 U.S.C. § 627]. Notices to be posted

Every employer, employment agency, and labor organization shall post and keep posted in conspicuous places upon its premises a notice to be prepared or approved by the Equal Employment Opportunity Commission setting forth information as the Commission deems appropriate to effectuate the purposes of this chapter.

Sec. 9 [29 U.S.C. § 628]. Rules and regulations; exemptions

In accordance with the provisions of subchapter II of chapter 5 of title 5, the Equal Employment Opportunity Commission may issue such rules and regulations as it may consider necessary or appropriate for carrying out this chapter, and may establish such reasonable exemptions to and from any or all provisions of this chapter as it may find necessary and proper in the public interest.[9]

Sec. 10 [29 U.S.C. § 629]. Criminal penalties

Whoever shall forcibly resist, oppose, impede, intimidate, or interfere with a duly authorized representative of the Equal Employment Opportunity Commission while it is engaged in the performance of duties under this chapter shall be punished by a fine of not more than $500 or by imprisonment for not more than one year, or by both:

9. Sections 104 and 105 of the Older Workers Benefit Protection Act of 1990, Pub.L.No. 101–433, 104 Stat. 981 (1990), codified as a Note to § 623, state:

Sec. 104. Rules and Regulations.

Notwithstanding section 9 of the Age Discrimination in Employment Act of 1967 (29 U.S.C. § 628), the Equal Employment Opportunity Commission may issue such rules and regulations as the Commission may consider necessary or appropriate for carrying out this title, and the amendments made by this title, only after consultation with the Secretary of the Treasury and the Secretary of Labor.

Provided, however, That no person shall be imprisoned under this section except when there has been a prior conviction hereunder.

Sec. 11 [29 U.S.C. § 630]. Definitions

For the purposes of this chapter—

(a) The term "person" means one or more individuals, partnerships, associations, labor organizations, corporations, business trust, legal representatives, or any organized groups of persons.

(b) The term "employer" means a person engaged in an industry affecting commerce who has twenty or more employees for each working day in each of twenty or more calendar weeks in the current or preceding calendar year: *Provided,* That prior to June 30, 1968, employers having fewer than fifty employees shall not be considered employers. The term also means (1) any agent of such a person, and (2) a State or political subdivision of a State and any agency or instrumentality of a State or a political subdivision of a State, and any interstate agency, but such term does not include the United States, or a corporation wholly owned by the Government of the United States.

(c) The term "employment agency" means any person regularly undertaking with or without compensation to procure employees for an employer and includes an agent of such a person; but shall not include an agency of the United States.

(d) The term "labor organization" means a labor organization engaged in an industry affecting commerce, and any agent of such an organization, and includes any organization of any kind, any agency, or employee representation committee, group, association, or plan so engaged in which employees participate and which exists for the purpose, in whole or in part, of dealing with employers concerning grievances, labor disputes, wages, rates of pay, hours, or other terms or conditions of employment, and any conference, general committee, joint or system board, or joint council so engaged which is subordinate to a national or international labor organization.

(e) A labor organization shall be deemed to be engaged in an industry affecting commerce if (1) it maintains or operates a hiring hall or hiring office which procures employees for an employer or procures for employees opportunities to work for an employer, or (2) the number of its members (or, where it is a labor organization composed of other labor organizations or their representatives, if the aggregate number of the members of such other labor organization) is fifty or more prior to July 1, 1968, or twenty-five or more on or after July 1, 1968, and such labor organization—

(1) is the certified representative of employees under the provisions of the National Labor Relations Act, as amended [29 U.S.C. § 151 et seq.], or the Railway Labor Act, as amended [45 U.S.C. § 151 et seq.]; or

(2) although not certified, is a national or international labor organization or a local labor organization recognized or acting as the representative of employees of an employer or employers engaged in an industry affecting commerce; or

(3) has chartered a local labor organization or subsidiary body which is representing or actively seeking to represent employees of employers within the meaning of paragraph (1) or (2); or

(4) has been chartered by a labor organization representing or actively seeking to represent employees within the meaning of paragraph (1) or (2) as the local or subordinate body through which such employees may enjoy membership or become affiliated with such labor organization; or

(5) is a conference, general committee, joint or system board, or joint council subordinate to a national or international labor organization, which includes a labor organization engaged in an industry affecting commerce within the meaning of any of the preceding paragraphs of this subsection.

(f) The term "employee" means an individual employed by any employer except that the term "employee" shall not include any person elected to public office in any State or political subdivision of any State by the qualified voters thereof, or any person chosen by such officer to be on such officer's personal staff, or an appointee on the policymaking level or an immediate adviser with respect to the exercise of the constitutional or legal powers of the office. The exemption set forth in the preceding sentence shall not include employees subject to the civil service laws of a State government, governmental agency, or political subdivision. The term "employee" includes any individual who is a citizen of the United States employed by an employer in a workplace in a foreign country.

(g) The term "commerce" means trade, traffic, commerce, transportation, transmission, or communication among the several States; or between a State and any place outside thereof; or within the District of Columbia, or a possession of the United States; or between points in the same State but through a point outside thereof.

(h) The term "industry affecting commerce" means any activity, business, or industry in commerce or in which a labor dispute would hinder or obstruct commerce or the free flow of commerce and includes any activity or industry "affecting commerce" within the meaning of the Labor–Management Reporting and Disclosure Act of 1959 [29 U.S.C. § 401 et seq.].

(i) The term "State" includes a State of the United States, the District of Columbia, Puerto Rico, the Virgin Islands, American Samoa, Guam, Wake Island, the Canal Zone, and Outer Continental Shelf lands defined in the Outer Continental Shelf Lands Act [43 U.S.C. § 1331 et seq.].

(j) The term "firefighter" means an employee, the duties of whose position are primarily to perform work directly connected with the control and extinguishment of fires or the maintenance and use of firefighting apparatus and equipment, including an employee engaged in this activity who is transferred to a supervisory or administrative position.

(k) The term "law enforcement officer" means an employee, the duties of whose position are primarily the investigation, apprehension, or detention of individuals suspected or convicted of offenses against the criminal laws of a State, including an employee engaged in this activity who is transferred to a supervisory or administrative position. For the purpose of this subsection, "detention" includes the duties of employees assigned to guard individuals incarcerated in any penal institution.

(*l*) The term "compensation, terms, conditions, or privileges of employment" encompasses all employee benefits, including such benefits provided pursuant to a bona fide employee benefit plan.[10]

Sec. 12 [29 U.S.C. § 631]. Age limits

(a) Individuals at least 40 years of age

The prohibitions in this chapter shall be limited to individuals who are at least 40 years of age.

(b) Employees or applicants for employment in Federal Government

In the case of any personnel action affecting employees or applicants for employment which is subject to the provisions of section 633a of this title, the prohibitions established in section 633a of this title shall be limited to individuals who are at least 40 years of age.

(c) Bona fide executives or high policymakers

(1) Nothing in this chapter shall be construed to prohibit compulsory retirement of any employee who has attained 65 years of age but not 70 years of age, and who, for the 2-year period immediately before retirement, is employed in a bona fide executive or a high policymaking position, if such employee is entitled to an immediate nonforfeitable annual retirement benefit from a pension, profit-sharing, savings, or deferred compensation plan, or any combination of such plans, of the employer of such employee, which equals, in the aggregate, at least $44,000.

(2) In applying the retirement benefit test of paragraph (1) of this subsection, if any such retirement benefit is in a form other than a straight life annuity (with no ancillary benefits), or if employees contribute to any such plan or make rollover contributions, such benefit shall be adjusted in accordance with regulations prescribed by the Equal Employ-

10. Section 11(*l*) was added pursuant to the Older Workers Benefit Protection Act of 1990. Pub.L.No. 101–433, 104 Stat. 978 (1990).

ment Opportunity Commission, after consultation with the Secretary of the Treasury, so that the benefit is the equivalent of a straight life annuity (with no ancillary benefits) under a plan to which employees do not contribute and under which no rollover contributions are made.

Sec. 13 [29 U.S.C. § 632]. Annual report to Congress

The Equal Employment Opportunity Commission shall submit annually in January a report to the Congress covering activities for the preceding year and including such information, data and recommendations for further legislation in connection with the matters covered by this chapter as it may find advisable. Such report shall contain an evaluation and appraisal by the Commission of the effect of the minimum and maximum ages established by this chapter, together with its recommendations to the Congress. In making such evaluation and appraisal, the Commission shall take into consideration any changes which may have occurred in the general age level of the population, the effect of the chapter upon workers not covered by its provisions, and such other factors as it may deem pertinent.

Sec. 14 [29 U.S.C. § 633]. Federal–State relationship

(a) Federal action superseding State action

Nothing in this chapter shall affect the jurisdiction of any State performing like functions with regard to discriminatory employment practices on account of age except that upon commencement of action under this chapter such action shall supersede any State action.

(b) Limitation of federal action upon commencement of state proceedings

In the case of an alleged unlawful practice occurring in a State which has a law prohibiting discrimination in employment because of age and establishing or authorizing a State authority to grant or seek relief from such discriminatory practice, no suit may be brought under section 626 of this title before the expiration of sixty days after proceedings have been commenced under the State law, unless such proceedings have been earlier terminated: *Provided*, That such sixty-day period shall be extended to one hundred and twenty days during the first year after the effective date of such State law. If any requirement for the commencement of such proceedings is imposed by a State authority other than a requirement of the filing of a written and signed statement of the facts upon which the proceeding is based, the proceeding shall be deemed to have been commenced for the purposes of this subsection at the time such statement is sent by registered mail to the appropriate State authority.

Sec. 15 [29 U.S.C. § 633a]. Nondiscrimination on account of age in Federal Government employment

(a) Federal agencies affected

All personnel actions affecting employees or applicants for employment who are at least 40 years of age (except personnel actions with regard to aliens employed outside the limits of the United States) in military departments as defined in section 102 of title 5, in executive agencies as defined in section 105 of title 5 (including employees and applicants for employment who are paid from nonappropriated funds), in the United States Postal Service and the Postal Rate Commission, in those units in the government of the District of Columbia having positions in the competitive service, and in those units of the legislative and judicial branches of the Federal Government having positions in the competitive service, and in the Government Printing Office, the General Accounting Office, and the Library of Congress shall be made free from any discrimination based on age.

(b) Enforcement by Equal Employment Opportunity Commission and by Librarian of Congress in the Library of Congress; remedies; rules, regulations; orders, and instructions of Commission; compliance by Federal agencies; powers and duties of Commission; notification of final action on complaint of discrimination; exemptions: bona fide occupational qualification

Except as otherwise provided in this subsection, the Equal Employment Opportunity Commission is authorized to enforce the provisions of subsection (a) of this subsection through appropriate remedies, including reinstatement or hiring of employees with or without backpay, as will effectuate the policies of this section. The Equal Employment Opportunity Commission shall issue such rules, regulations, orders, and instructions as it deems necessary and appropriate to carry out its responsibilities under this section. The Equal Employment Opportunity Commission shall—

(1) be responsible for the review and evaluation of the operation of all agency programs designed to carry out the policy of this section, periodically obtaining and publishing (on at least a semiannual basis) progress reports from each department, agency, or unit referred to in subsection (a) of this section;

(2) consult with and solicit the recommendations of interested individuals, groups, and organizations relating to nondiscrimination in employment on account of age; and

(3) provide for the acceptance and processing of complaints of discrimination in Federal employment on account of age.

The head of each department, agency, or unit shall comply with such rules, regulations, orders, and instructions of the Equal Employment Opportunity Commission which shall include a provision that an employee or applicant for employment shall be notified of any final action taken on any complaint of discrimination filed by him thereunder. Reasonable exemptions to the provisions of this section may be established by the Commission but only when the Commission has established a maximum age requirement on the basis of a determination that age is a bona fide occupational qualification necessary to the performance of the duties of the position. With respect to employment in the Library of Congress, authorities granted in this subsection to the Equal Employment Opportunity Commission shall be exercised by the Librarian of Congress.

(c) Civil action: jurisdiction; relief

Any person aggrieved may bring a civil action in any Federal district court of competent jurisdiction for such legal or equitable relief as will effectuate the purposes of this chapter.

(d) Notice to the Commission; time of notice; Commission notification of prospective defendants; Commission elimination of unlawful practices

When the individual has not filed a complaint concerning age discrimination with the commission, no civil action may be commenced by any individual under this section until the individual has given the Commission not less than thirty days' notice of an intent to file such action. Such notice shall be filed within one hundred and eighty days after the alleged unlawful practice occurred. Upon receiving a notice of intent to sue, the Commission shall promptly notify all persons named therein as prospective defendants in the action and take any appropriate action to assure the elimination of any unlawful practice.

(e) Duty of government agency or official

Nothing contained in this section shall relieve any Government agency or official of the responsibility to assure nondiscrimination on account of age in employment as required under any provision of Federal law.

(f) Applicability of statutory provisions to personnel action of Federal departments, etc.

Any personnel action of any department, agency, or other entity referred to in subsection (a) of this section shall not be subject to, or affected by, any provision of this chapter, other than the provisions of ***sections 626(d)(3) and*** 631(b) of this title and the provisions of this section.

(g) Study and report to President and Congress by Equal Employment Opportunity Commission, etc.

(1) The Equal Employment Opportunity Commission shall undertake a study relating to the effects of the amendments made to this section by the Age Discrimination in Employment Act Amendments of 1978, and the effects of section 631(b) of this title.

(2) The Equal Employment Opportunity Commission shall transmit a report to the President and to the Congress containing the findings of the Commission resulting from the study of the Commission under paragraph (1) of this subsection. Such report shall be transmitted no later than January 1, 1980.

VOCATIONAL REHABILITATION ACT OF 1973
29 U.S.C. §§ 705, 791, 793–794a

§ 705 [§ 7]. Definitions

For the purposes of this chapter:

* * *

(9) Disability[1]

The term "disability" means—

(A) except as otherwise provided in subparagraph (B), a physical or mental impairment that constitutes or results in a substantial impediment to employment; or

(B) for purposes of sections 701, 711, and 712 of this title and subchapters II, IV, V, and VII of this chapter, *the meaning given it in section 12102 of Title 42* [*section 3 of the Americans with Disabilities Act of 1990*].[2]

(10)(A) The term "drug" means a controlled substance, as defined in schedules I through V of section 202 of the Controlled Substances Act [21 U.S.C. § 812].

(B) The term "illegal use of drugs" means the use of drugs, the possession or distribution of which is unlawful under the Controlled Substances Act [21 U.S.C. § 801 et seq.]. Such term does not include the use of a drug taken under supervision by a licensed health care professional, or other uses authorized by the Controlled Substances Act or other provision of Federal law.

* * *

(20)(A) Except as otherwise provided in subparagraph (B), the term "individual with a disability" means any individual who—

(i) has a physical or mental impairment which for such individual constitutes or results in a substantial impediment to employment; and

(ii) can benefit in terms of employment from vocational rehabilitation services provided pursuant to titles I, III, or VI of this chapter.

(B) Subject to subchapters (C), (D), (E), and (F), the term "individual with a disability" means, for purposes of sections 701, 711, and 712 of this title, and subchapters II, IV, V and VII of this chapter, *any person*

1. Congress substituted the term "disability" for the term "handicap" in the 1992 amendments to the Rehabilitation Act. The original Act had used the term "handicap." Pub.L.No. 102–569, 106 Stat. 4346 (1992).

2. In § 7 of the ADA Amendments Act of 2008, Pub.L.No. 110–325, 122 Stat. 3553 (2008), Congress substituted the language in italics for "a physical or mental impairment that substantially limits one or more major life activities."

who has a disability as defined in section 12102 of Title 42 [section 3 of the Americans with Disabilities Act of 1990].

(C)(i) For purposes of subchapter V of this chapter, the term "individual with a disability" does not include any individual who is currently engaging in the illegal use of drugs, when a covered entity acts on the basis of such use.

(ii) Nothing in clause (i) shall be construed to exclude as an individual with a disability an individual who—

(I) has successfully completed a supervised drug rehabilitation program and is no longer engaging in the illegal use of drugs, or has otherwise been rehabilitated successfully and is no longer engaging in such use;

(II) is participating in a supervised rehabilitation program and is no longer engaging in such use; or

(III) is erroneously regarded as engaging in such use, but is not engaging in such use;

except that it shall not be a violation of this chapter for a covered entity to adopt or administer reasonable policies or procedures, including but not limited to drug testing, designed to ensure that an individual described in subclause (I) or (II) is no longer engaging in the illegal use of drugs.

(iii) Notwithstanding clause (i), for purposes of programs and activities providing health services and services provided under subchapters I, II and III of this chapter, an individual shall not be excluded from the benefits of such programs or activities on the basis of his or her current illegal use of drugs if he or she is otherwise entitled to such services.

(iv) For purposes of programs and activities providing educational services, local educational agencies may take disciplinary action pertaining to the use or possession of illegal drugs or alcohol against any student who is an individual with a disability and who currently is engaging in the illegal use of drugs or in the use of alcohol to the same extent that such disciplinary action is taken against students who are not individuals with disabilities. Furthermore, the due process procedures at 34 C.F.R. 104.36 shall not apply to such disciplinary actions.

(v) For purposes of sections 793 and 794 of this title as such sections relate to employment, the term "individual with a disability" does not include any individual who is an alcoholic whose current use of alcohol prevents such individual from performing the duties of the job in question or whose employment, by reason of such current alcohol abuse, would constitute a direct threat to property or the safety of others.

(D) For the purposes of sections 793 and 794 of this title, as such sections relate to employment, such term does not include an individual who has a currently contagious disease or infection and who, by reason of such disease or infection, would constitute a direct threat to the health or safety of other individuals or who, by reason of the currently contagious disease or infection, is unable to perform the duties of the job.

(E) For purposes of section 791, 793, and 794 of this title—

(i) for purposes of the application of subparagraph (B) to such sections, the term "impairment" does not include homosexuality or bisexuality; and

(ii) therefore the term "individual with a disability" does not include an individual on the basis of homosexuality or bisexuality.

(F) For the purposes of sections 791, 793, and 794 of this title, the term "individual with a disability" does not include an individual on the basis of—

(i) transvestism, transsexualism, pedophilia, exhibitionism, voyeurism, gender identity disorders not resulting from physical impairments, or other sexual behavior disorders;

(ii) compulsive gambling, kleptomania, or pyromania; or

(iii) psychoactive substance use disorders resulting from current illegal use of drugs.

* * *

§ 791 [§ 501]. Employment of individuals with disabilities Federal Agencies; affirmative action program plans

* * *

(b) Each department, agency, and instrumentality (including the United States Postal Service and the Postal Rate Commission) in the executive branch shall, within one hundred and eighty days after September 26, 1973, submit to the [Equal Employment Opportunity] Commission and to the Committee an affirmative action program plan for the hiring, placement, and advancement of individuals with a disabilities in such department, agency, or instrumentality. Such plan shall include a description of the extent to which and methods whereby the special needs of employees who are individuals with disabilities are being met. Such plan shall be updated annually, and shall be reviewed annually by the Commission, if the Commission determines, after consultation with the Committee, that such plan provides sufficient assurances, procedures and commitments to provide adequate hiring, placement, and advancement opportunities for individuals with disabilities.

* * *

§ 793 [§ 503]. Employment under Federal contracts

(a) Amount of contracts or subcontracts; provision for employment and advancement of qualified individuals with disabilities; regulations

Any contract in excess of $10,000 entered into by any Federal department or agency for the procurement of personal property and nonpersonal services (including construction) for the United States shall contain a provision requiring that the party contracting with the United States shall take affirmative action to employ and advance in employment qualified individuals with disabilities. The provisions of this section shall apply to any subcontract in excess of $10,000 entered into by a prime contractor in carrying out any contract for the procurement of personal property and nonpersonal services (including construction) for the United States. The President shall implement the provisions of this section by promulgating regulations within ninety days after September 26, 1973.

(b) Administrative enforcement; complaints; investigations; departmental action

If any individual with a disability believes any contractor has failed or refused to comply with the provisions of his contract with the United States, relating to employment of individuals with disabilities, such individual may file a complaint with the Department of Labor. The Department shall promptly investigate such complaint and shall take such action thereon as the facts and circumstances warrant, consistent with the terms of such contract and the laws and regulations applicable thereto.

(c) Waiver by President; national interest circumstances for waiver of particular agreements; waiver by Secretary of Labor of affirmative action requirements

(1) The requirements of this section may be waived, in whole or in part, by the President with respect to a particular contract or subcontract, in accordance with guidelines set forth in regulations which the President shall prescribe, when the President determines that special circumstances in the national interest so require and states in writing the reasons for such determination.

* * *

§ 794 [§ 504]. Nondiscrimination under Federal grants and programs

(a) Promulgation of rules and regulations

No otherwise qualified individual with a disability in the United States, as defined in section 706(8) of this title, shall, solely by reason of her or his disability, be excluded from the participation in, be denied the benefits of, or be subjected to discrimination under any program or activity receiving Federal financial assistance or under any program or activity conducted by any Executive agency or by the United States Postal Service. The head of each such agency shall promulgate such regulations as may be necessary to carry out the amendments to this section made by the Rehabilitation, Comprehensive Services, and Developmental Disabilities Act of 1978. Copies of any proposed regulation shall be submitted to appropriate authorizing committees of the Congress, and such regulation may take effect no earlier than the thirtieth day after the date on which regulation is so submitted to such committees.

(b) "Program or activity" defined

For the purposes of this section, the term "program or activity" means all of the operations of—

(1)(A) a department, agency, special purpose district, other instrumentality of a State or local government; or

(B) the entity of such State or local government that distributes such assistance and each such department or agency (and each other State or local government entity) to which the assistance is extended, in the case of assistance to a State or local government;

(2)(A) a college, university, or other postsecondary institution, or a public system of higher education; or

(B) a local educational agency (as defined in section 8801 of title 20), system of vocational education, or other school system;

(3)(A) an entire corporation, partnership, or private organization, or entire sole proprietorship—

(i) if assistance is extended to such corporation, partnership, private organization, or sole proprietorship as a whole; or

(ii) which is principally engaged in the business of providing education, health care, housing, social services, or parks and recreation; or

(B) the entire plant or other comparable, geographically separate facility to which Federal financial assistance is extended, in the case of any other corporation, partnership, private organization, or sole proprietorship; or

(4) any other entity which is established by two or more of the entities described in paragraphs (1), (2), or (3); any part of which is extended Federal financial assistance.

(c) Significant structural alterations by small providers

Small providers are not required by subsection (a) of this section to make significant structural alterations to their existing facilities for the purpose of assuring program accessibility, if alternative means of providing the services are available. The terms used in this subsection shall be construed with reference to the regulations existing on March 22, 1988.

(d) Standards used in determining violation of section

The standards used to determine whether this section has been violated in a complaint alleging employment discrimination under this section shall be the standards applied under title I of the Americans with Disabilities Act of 1990 [42 U.S.C. § 12111 et seq.] and provisions of sections 501 through 504, and 510 of the Americans with Disabilities Act of 1990 [42 U.S.C. §§ 12201–12204 and 12210], as such sections relate to employment.

§ 794a [§ 505]. Remedies and attorney fees

(a)(1) The remedies, procedures, and rights set forth in section 717 of the Civil Rights Act of 1964 [42 U.S.C. § 2000e–16], including the application of sections 706(f) through 706(k) [42 U.S.C. §§ 2000e–5(f) through (k)] (and the application of section 706(e)(3) [42 U.S.C. § 2000e–5(e)(3)] to claims of discrimination in compensation), shall be available, with respect to any complaint under section 791 this title, to any employee or applicant for employment aggrieved by the final disposition of such complaint, or by the failure to take final action on such complaint. In fashioning an equitable or affirmative action remedy under such section, a court may take into account the reasonableness of the cost of any necessary work place accommodation, and the availability of alternatives therefor or other appropriate relief in order to achieve an equitable and appropriate remedy.

(2) The remedies, procedures, and rights set forth in title VI of the Civil Rights Act of 1964 [42 U.S.C. § 2000d et seq.] shall be available to any person aggrieved by any act or failure to act by any recipient of Federal assistance or Federal provider of such assistance under section 794 of this title.

(b) In any action or proceeding to enforce or charge a violation of a provision of this subchapter, the court, in its discretion, may allow the prevailing party, other than the United States, a reasonable attorney's fee as part of the costs.

AMERICANS WITH DISABILITIES ACT OF 1990
42 U.S.C. §§ 12101–12102, 12111–12117, 12201–12213

Sec. 2 [42 U.S.C. § 12101]. Findings and purposes

(a) Findings

The Congress finds that—

(1) *physical or mental disabilities in no way diminish a person's right to fully participate in all aspects of society, yet many people with physical or mental disabilities have been precluded from doing so because of discrimination; others who have a record of a disability or are regarded as having a disability also have been subjected to discrimination;*[1]

(2) historically, society has tended to isolate and segregate individuals with disabilities, and, despite some improvements, such forms of discrimination against individuals with disabilities continue to be a serious and pervasive social problem;

(3) discrimination against individuals with disabilities persists in such critical areas as employment, housing, public accommodations, education, transportation, communication, recreation, institutionalization, health services, voting, and access to public services;

(4) unlike individuals who have experienced discrimination on the basis of race, color, sex, national origin, religion, or age, individuals who have experienced discrimination on the basis of disability have often had no legal recourse to redress such discrimination;

(5) individuals with disabilities continually encounter various forms of discrimination, including outright intentional exclusion, the discriminatory effects of architectural, transportation, and communication barriers, overprotective rules and policies, failure to make modifications to existing facilities and practices, exclusionary qualification standards and criteria, segregation, and relegation to lesser services, programs, activities, benefits, jobs, or other opportunities;

(6) census data, national polls, and other studies have documented that people with disabilities, as a group, occupy an inferior status in our society, and are severely disadvantaged socially, vocationally, economically, and educationally;

1. The text in italics in § 2(a)(1) was amended by § 3(1) of the ADA Amendments Act of 2008, Pub.L.No. 110–325, 122 Stat. 3553 (2008). Subsection (a)(1) formerly read: "(1) some 43,000,000 Americans have one or more physical or mental disabilities, and this number is increasing as the population as a whole is growing older".

(7) the Nation's proper goals regarding individuals with disabilities are to assure equality of opportunity, full participation, independent living, and economic self-sufficiency for such individuals; and[2]

(8) the continuing existence of unfair and unnecessary discrimination and prejudice denies people with disabilities the opportunity to compete on an equal basis and to pursue those opportunities for which our free society is justifiably famous, and costs the United States billions of dollars in unnecessary expenses resulting from dependency and nonproductivity.

(9) Redesignated (8).

(b) Purpose

It is the purpose of this chapter—

(1) to provide a clear and comprehensive national mandate for the elimination of discrimination against individuals with disabilities;

(2) to provide clear, strong, consistent, enforceable standards addressing discrimination against individuals with disabilities;

(3) to ensure that the Federal Government plays a central role in enforcing the standards established in this chapter on behalf of individuals with disabilities; and

(4) to invoke the sweep of congressional authority; including its power to enforce the fourteenth amendment and to regulate commerce, in order to address the major areas of discrimination faced day-to-day by people with disabilities.

Sec. 3 [42 U.S.C. § 12102]. Definition of disability[3]

As used in this chapter:

(1) Disability

The term "disability" means, with respect to an individual—

(A) a physical or mental impairment that substantially limits one or more major life activities of such individual;

(B) a record of such an impairment; or

(C) being regarded as having such an impairment (as described in paragraph (3)).

2. Section 3(2)–(3) of the ADA Amendments Act of 2008, Pub.L.No. 110–325, 122 Stat. 3553 (2008), struck out paragraph (7) and renumbered former paragraphs (8) and (9) as paragraphs (7) and (8), respectively. The deleted text in former paragraph (7) had read: "(7) individuals with disabilities are a discrete and insular minority who have been faced with restrictions and limitations, subjected to a history of purposeful unequal treatment, and relegated to a position of political powerlessness in our society, based on characteristics that are beyond the control of such individuals and resulting from stereotypic assumptions not truly indicative of the individual ability of such individuals to participate in, and contribute to, society".

3. The text printed in italics in § 3 was added by § 4 of the ADA Amendments Act of 2008, Pub.L.No. 110–325, 122 Stat. 3553 (2008).

(2) Major life activities

(A) *In general*

For purposes of paragraph (1), major life activities include, but are not limited to caring for oneself, performing manual tasks, seeing, hearing, eating, sleeping, walking, standing, lifting, bending, speaking, breathing, learning, reading, concentrating, thinking, communicating, and working.

(B) *Major bodily functions*

For purposes of paragraph (1), a major life activity also includes the operation of a major bodily function, including but not limited to, functions of the immune system, normal cell growth, digestive, bowel, bladder, neurological, brain, respiratory, circulatory, endocrine, and reproductive functions.

(3) Regarded as having such an impairment

For purposes of paragraph (1)(C):

(A) *An individual meets the requirement of "being regarded as having such an impairment" if the individual establishes that he or she has been subjected to an action prohibited under this chapter because of an actual or perceived physical or mental impairment whether or not the impairment limits or is perceived to limit a major life activity.*

(B) *Paragraph (1)(C) shall not apply to impairments that are transitory and minor. A transitory impairment is an impairment with an actual or expected duration of 6 months or less.*

(4) Rules of construction regarding the definition of disability

The definition of "disability" in paragraph (1) shall be construed in accordance with the following:

(A) *The definition of disability in this chapter shall be construed in favor of broad coverage of individuals under this chapter, to the maximum extent permitted by the terms of this chapter.*

(B) *The term "substantially limits" shall be interpreted consistently with the findings and purposes of the ADA Amendments Act of 2008.*

(C) *An impairment that substantially limits one major life activity need not limit other major life activities in order to be considered a disability.*

(D) *An impairment that is episodic or in remission is a disability if it would substantially limit a major life activity when active.*

(E)(i) *The determination of whether an impairment substantially limits a major life activity shall be made without regard to the ameliorative effects of mitigating measures such as—*

(I) *medication, medical supplies, equipment, or appliances, low-vision devices (which do not include ordinary eyeglasses or contact lenses), prosthetics including limbs and devices, hearing aids and cochlear implants or other implantable hearing devices, mobility devices, or oxygen therapy equipment and supplies;*

(II) *use of assistive technology;*

(III) *reasonable accommodations or auxiliary aids or services; or*

(IV) *learned behavioral or adaptive neurological modifications.*

(ii) *The ameliorative effects of the mitigating measures of ordinary eyeglasses or contact lenses shall be considered in determining whether an impairment substantially limits a major life activity.*

(iii) *As used in this subparagraph—*

(I) *the term "ordinary eyeglasses or contact lenses" means lenses that are intended to fully correct visual acuity or eliminate refractive error; and*

(II) *the term "low-vision devices" means devices that magnify, enhance, or otherwise augment a visual image.*

Sec. 4 [42 U.S.C. § 12103]. Additional definitions[4]

As used in this chapter:

(1) Auxiliary aids and services

The term "auxiliary aids and services" includes—

(A) qualified interpreters or other effective methods of making aurally delivered materials available to individuals with hearing impairments;

(B) qualified readers, taped texts, or other effective methods of making visually delivered materials available to individuals with visual impairments;

(C) acquisition or modification of equipment or devices; and

(D) other similar services and actions.

(2) State

The term "State" means each of the several States, the District of Columbia, the Commonwealth of Puerto Rico, Guam, American Samoa, the Virgin Islands of the United States, the Trust Territory of the Pacific Islands, and the Commonwealth of the Northern Mariana Islands.

* * *

4. Section 4, which was formerly § 3, was renumbered by the ADA Amendments Act of 2008.

TITLE I—EMPLOYMENT

Sec. 101 [42 U.S.C. § 12111]. Definitions

As used in this subchapter:

(1) Commission

The term "Commission" means the Equal Employment Opportunity Commission established by section 2000e–4 of this title.

(2) Covered Entity

The term "covered entity" means an employer, employment agency, labor organization, or joint labor-management committee.

(3) Direct Threat

The term "direct threat" means a significant risk to the health or safety of others that cannot be eliminated by reasonable accommodation.

(4) Employee

The term "employee" means an individual employed by an employer. With respect to employment in a foreign country, such term includes an individual who is a citizen of the United States.[5]

(5) Employer

(A) In general

The term "employer" means a person engaged in an industry affecting commerce who has 15 or more employees for each working day in each of 20 or more calendar weeks in the current or preceding calendar year, and any agent of such person, except that, for two years following the effective date of this subchapter, an employer means a person engaged in an industry affecting commerce who has 25 or more employees for each working day in each of 20 or more calendar weeks in the current or preceding year, and any agent of such person.

(B) Exceptions

The term "employer" does not include—

(i) the United States, a corporation wholly owned by the government of the United States, or an Indian tribe; or

(ii) a bona fide private membership club (other than a labor organization) that is exempt from taxation under section 501(c) of title 26 [Internal Revenue Code of 1986].

(6) Illegal use of drugs

(A) In general

The term "illegal use of drugs" means the use of drugs, the possession or distribution of which is unlawful under the Controlled Substances Act [21 U.S.C. § 801 et seq.]. Such term does not include

5. The last sentence was added by the Civil Rights Act of 1991, Pub.L.No. 102–166, § 109(a), 105 Stat. 1071 (1991).

the use of a drug taken under supervision by a licensed health care professional, or other uses authorized by the Controlled Substances Act or other provisions of Federal law.

(B) Drugs

The term "drug" means a controlled substance, as defined in schedules I through V of section 202 of the Controlled Substances Act [21 U.S.C. § 812].

(7) Person, etc.

The terms "person," "labor organization," "employment agency," "commerce," and "industry affecting commerce," shall have the same meaning given such terms in section 2000e of this title [Title VII Civil Rights Act of 1964].

(8) Qualified individual

The term "qualified individual" means an individual who, with or without reasonable accommodation, can perform the essential functions of the employment position that such individual holds or desires. For the purposes of this subchapter, consideration shall be given to the employer's judgment as to what functions of a job are essential, and if an employer has prepared a written description before advertising or interviewing applicants for the job, this description shall be considered evidence of the essential functions of the job.

(9) Reasonable Accommodation

The term "reasonable accommodation" may include—

(A) making existing facilities used by employees readily accessible to and usable by individuals with disabilities; and

(B) job restructuring, part-time or modified work schedules, reassignment to a vacant position, acquisition or modification of equipment or devices, appropriate adjustment or modifications of examinations, training materials or policies, the provision of qualified readers or interpreters, and other similar accommodations for individuals with disabilities.

(10) Undue hardship

(A) In general

The term "undue hardship" means an action requiring significant difficulty or expense, when considered in light of the factors set forth in subparagraph (B).

(B) Factors to be considered

In determining whether an accommodation would impose an undue hardship on a covered entity, factors to be considered include—

(i) the nature and cost of the accommodation needed under this chapter;

(ii) the overall financial resources of the facility or facilities involved in the provision of the reasonable accommodation; the number of persons employed at such facility; the effect on expenses and resources, or the impact otherwise of such accommodation upon the operation of the facility;

(iii) the overall financial resources of the covered entity; the overall size of the business of a covered entity with respect to the number of its employees; the number, type, and location of its facilities; and

(iv) the type of operation or operations of the covered entity, including the composition, structure, and functions of the workforce of such entity; the geographic separateness, administrative, or fiscal relationship of the facility or facilities in question to the covered entity.

Sec. 102 [42 U.S.C. § 12112]. Discrimination

(a) General Rule

No covered entity shall discriminate against a qualified individual *on the basis of disability* in regard to job application procedures, the hiring, advancement, or discharge of employees, employee compensation, job training, and other terms, conditions, and privileges of employment.

(b) Construction

As used in subsection (a) of this section, the term "discriminate *against a qualified individual on the basis of disability*" includes—

(1) limiting, segregating, or classifying a job applicant or employee in a way that adversely affects the opportunities or status of such applicant or employee because of the disability of such applicant or employee;

(2) participating in a contractual or other arrangement or relationship that has the effect of subjecting a covered entity's qualified applicant or employee with a disability to the discrimination prohibited by this subchapter (such relationship includes a relationship with an employment or referral agency, labor union, an organization providing fringe benefits to an employee of the covered entity, or an organization providing training and apprenticeship programs);

(3) utilizing standards, criteria, or methods of administration—

(A) that have the effect of discrimination on the basis of disability; or

(B) that perpetuate the discrimination of others who are subject to common administrative control;

(4) excluding or otherwise denying equal jobs or benefits to a qualified individual because of the known disability of an individual with whom the qualified individual is known to have a relationship or association;

(5)(A) not making reasonable accommodations to the known physical or mental limitations of an otherwise qualified individual with a disability who is an applicant or employee, unless such covered entity can demonstrate that the accommodation would impose an undue hardship on the operation of the business of such covered entity; or

(B) denying employment opportunities to a job applicant or employee who is an otherwise qualified individual with a disability, if such denial is based on the need of such covered entity to make reasonable accommodation to the physical or mental impairments of the employee or applicant;

(6) using qualification standards, employment tests or other selection criteria that screen out or tend to screen out an individual with a disability or a class of individuals with disabilities unless the standard, test or other selection criteria, as used by the covered entity, is shown to be job-related for the position in question and is consistent with business necessity; and

(7) failing to select and administer tests concerning employment in the most effective manner to ensure that, when such test is administered to a job applicant or employee who has a disability that impairs sensory, manual, or speaking skills, such test results accurately reflect the skills, aptitude, or whatever other factor of such applicant or employee that such test purports to measure, rather than reflecting the impaired sensory, manual, or speaking skills of such employee or applicant (except where such skills are the factors that the test purports to measure).

(c) Covered entities in foreign countries[6]

(1) In General

It shall not be unlawful under this section for a covered entity to take any action that constitutes discrimination under this section with respect to an employee in a workplace in a foreign country if compliance with this section would cause such covered entity to violate the law of the foreign country in which such workplace is located.

(2) Control of corporation

(A) Presumption

If an employer controls a corporation whose place of incorporation is a foreign country, any practice that constitutes discrimination under this section and is engaged in by such corporation shall be presumed to be engaged in by such employer.

(B) Exceptions

This section shall not apply with respect to the foreign operations of an employer that is a foreign person not controlled by an American employer.

6. Section 102(c) was added by the Civil Rights Act of 1991, Pub.L.No. 102–166, § 109(c)(2), 105 Stat. 1071 (1991).

(C) Determination

For purposes of this paragraph, the determination of whether an employer controls a corporation shall be based on—

(i) the interrelation of operations;

(ii) the common management;

(iii) the centralized control of labor relations; and

(iv) the common ownership or financial control, of the employer and the corporation.

(d) Medical examinations and inquiries—

(1) In general

The prohibition against discrimination as referred to in subsection (a) of this section shall include medical examinations and inquiries.

(2) Preemployment—

(A) Prohibited examination or inquiry

Except as provided in paragraph (3), a covered entity shall not conduct a medical examination or make inquiries of a job applicant as to whether such applicant is an individual with a disability or as to the nature or severity of such disability.

(B) Acceptable inquiry

A covered entity may make preemployment inquiries into the ability of an applicant to perform job-related functions.

(3) Employment entrance examination

A covered entity may require a medical examination after an offer of employment has been made to a job applicant and prior to the commencement of the employment duties of such applicant, and may condition an offer of employment on the results of such examination, if—

(A) all entering employees are subjected to such an examination regardless of disability;

(B) information obtained regarding the medical condition or history of the applicant is collected and maintained on separate forms and in separate medical files and is treated as a confidential medical record, except that—

(i) supervisors and managers may be informed regarding necessary restrictions on the work or duties of the employee and necessary accommodations;

(ii) first aid and safety personnel may be informed, when appropriate, if the disability might require emergency treatment; and

(iii) government officials investigating compliance with this chapter shall be provided relevant information on request; and

(C) the results of such examination are used only in accordance with this subchapter.

(4) Examination and inquiry

(A) Prohibited examinations and inquiries

A covered entity shall not require a medical examination and shall not make inquiries of an employee as to whether such an employee is an individual with a disability or as to the nature or severity of the disability, unless such examination or inquiry is shown to be job-related and consistent with business necessity.

(B) Acceptable examinations and inquiries

A covered entity may conduct voluntary medical examinations, including voluntary medical histories, which are part of an employee health program available to employees at that work site. A covered entity may make inquiries into the ability of an employee to perform job-related functions.

(C) Requirement

Information obtained under subparagraph (B) regarding the medical condition or history of any employee are subject to the requirements of subparagraphs (B) and (C) of paragraph (3).

Sec. 103 [42 U.S.C. § 12113]. Defenses

(a) In general

It may be a defense to a charge of discrimination under this chapter that an alleged application of qualification standards, tests, or selection criteria that screen out or tend to screen out or otherwise deny a job or benefit to an individual with a disability has been shown to be job-related and consistent with business necessity, and such performance cannot be accomplished by reasonable accommodation, as required under this subchapter.

(b) Qualification standards

The term "qualification standards" may include a requirement that an individual shall not pose a direct threat to the health or safety of other individuals in the workplace.

(c) Qualification standards and tests related to uncorrected vision[7]

Notwithstanding section 12102(4)(E)(ii) of this title, a covered entity shall not use qualification standards, employment tests, or other selection criteria based on an individual's uncorrected vision unless the standard, test, or other selection criteria, as used by the covered entity, is shown to be job-related for the position in question and consistent with business necessity.

7. Section (c), printed in italics, was added by § 5(b) of the ADA Amendments Act of 2008, Pub.L.No. 110–325, 122 Stat. 3553 (2008).

(d) Religious entities—

(1) In general

This subchapter shall not prohibit a religious corporation, association, educational institution, or society from giving preference in employment to individuals of a particular religion to perform work connected with the carrying on by such corporation, association, educational institution, or society of its activities.

(2) Religious tenets requirement

Under this subchapter, a religious organization may require that all applicants and employees conform to the religious tenets of such organization.

(e) List of infectious and communicable diseases

(1) In general

The Secretary of Health and Human Services, not later than 6 months after July 26, 1990, shall—

(A) review all infectious and communicable diseases which may be transmitted through handling the food supply;

(B) publish a list of infectious and communicable diseases which are transmitted through handling the food supply;

(C) publish the methods by which such diseases are transmitted; and

(D) widely disseminate such information regarding the list of diseases and their modes of transmissibility to the general public.

Such list shall be updated annually.

(2) Applications

In any case in which an individual has an infectious or communicable disease that is transmitted to others through the handling of food, that is included on the list developed by the Secretary of Health and Human Services under paragraph (1), and which cannot be eliminated by reasonable accommodation, a covered entity may refuse to assign or continue to assign such individual to a job involving food handling.

(3) Construction

Nothing in this Act shall be construed to preempt, modify, or amend any State, county, or local law, ordinance, or regulation applicable to food handling which is designed to protect the public health from individuals who pose a significant risk to the health or safety of others, which cannot be eliminated by reasonable accommodation, pursuant to the list of infectious or communicable diseases and the modes of transmissibility published by the Secretary of Health and Human Services.

Sec. 104 [42 U.S.C. § 12114]. Illegal use of drugs and alcohol

(a) Qualified individual with a disability

For purposes of this subchapter, "a qualified individual with a disability" shall not include any employee or applicant who is currently engaging in the illegal use of drugs, when the covered entity acts on the basis of such use.

(b) Rules of construction

Nothing in subsection (a) of this section shall be construed to exclude as a qualified individual with a disability an individual who—

(1) has successfully completed a supervised drug rehabilitation program and is no longer engaging in the illegal use of drugs, or has otherwise been rehabilitated successfully and is no longer engaging in such use;

(2) is participating in a supervised rehabilitation program and is no longer engaging in such use; or

(3) is erroneously regarded as engaging in such use, but is not engaging in such use;

except that it shall not be a violation of this chapter for a covered entity to adopt or administer reasonable policies or procedures, including but not limited to drug testing, designed to ensure that an individual described in paragraph (1) or (2) is no longer engaging in the illegal use of drugs.

(c) Authority of covered entity

A covered entity—

(1) may prohibit the illegal use of drugs and the use of alcohol at the workplace by all employees;

(2) may require that employees shall not be under the influence of alcohol or be engaging in the illegal use of drugs at the workplace;

(3) may require that employees behave in conformance with the requirements established under the Drug-Free Workplace Act of 1988 (41 U.S.C. § 701 et seq.);

(4) may hold an employee who engages in illegal use of drugs or who is an alcoholic to the same qualification standards for employment or job performance and behavior that such entity holds other employees, even if any unsatisfactory performance or behavior is related to the drug use or alcoholism of such employee; and

(5) may, with respect to Federal regulations regarding alcohol and the illegal use of drugs, require that—

(A) employees comply with the standards established in such regulations of the Department of Defense, if the employees of the covered entity are employed in an industry subject to such regulations, including complying with regulations (if any) that apply to employment in sensitive positions in such an industry, in the case of employees of the covered entity who are employed in such positions (as defined in the regulations of the Department of Defense);

(B) employees comply with the standards established in such regulations of the Nuclear Regulatory Commission, if the employees of the covered entity are employed in an industry subject to such regulations, including complying with regulations (if any) that apply to employment in sensitive positions in such an industry, in the case of employees of the covered entity who are employed in such positions (as defined in the regulations of the Nuclear Regulatory Commission); and

(C) employees comply with the standards established in such regulations of the Department of Transportation, if the employees of the covered entity are employed in a transportation industry subject to such regulations, including complying with such regulations (if any) that apply to employment in sensitive positions in such an industry, in the case of employees of the covered entity who are employed in such positions (as defined in the regulations of the Department of Transportation).

(d) Drug testing

(1) In general

For purposes of this subchapter, a test to determine the illegal use of drugs shall not be considered a medical examination.

(2) Construction

Nothing in this subchapter shall be construed to encourage, prohibit, or authorize the conducting of drug testing for the illegal use of drugs by job applicants or employees or making employment decisions based on such test results.

(e) Transportation Employees

Nothing in this subchapter shall be construed to encourage, prohibit, restrict, or authorize the otherwise lawful exercise by entities subject to the jurisdiction of the Department of Transportation of authority to—

(1) test employees of such entities in, and applicants for, positions involving safety-sensitive duties for the illegal use of drugs and for on-duty impairment by alcohol; and

(2) remove such persons who test positive for illegal use of drugs and on-duty impairment by alcohol pursuant to paragraph (1) from safety-sensitive duties in implementing subsection (c).

Sec. 105 [42 U.S.C. § 12115]. Posting notices

Every employer, employment agency, labor organization, or joint labor-management committee covered under this subchapter shall post notices in an accessible format to applicants, employees, and members describing the applicable provisions of this chapter, in the manner prescribed by section 711 of [Title VII of the Civil Rights Act of 1964, 42 U.S.C. § 2000e–10].

Sec. 106 [42 U.S.C. § 12116]. Regulations

Not later than 1 year after July 26, 1990, the Commission shall issue regulations in an accessible format to carry out this subchapter in accordance with subchapter II of chapter 5 of title 5.

Sec. 107 [42 U.S.C. § 12117]. Enforcement

(a) Powers, remedies, and procedures

The powers, remedies, and procedures set forth in sections 705, 706, 707, 709, and 710 of [Title VII of the Civil Rights Act of 1964, 42 U.S.C. §§ 2000e–4, 2000e–5, 2000e–6, 2000e–8, and 2000e–9] shall be the powers, remedies, and procedures this subchapter provides to the Commission, to the Attorney General, or to any person alleging discrimination on the basis of disability in violation of any provision of this chapter, or regulations promulgated under section 12116 of this title, concerning employment.

(b) Coordination

The agencies with enforcement authority for actions which allege employment discrimination under this subchapter and under the Rehabilitation Act of 1973 [29 U.S.C. § 701 et seq.] shall develop procedures to ensure that administrative complaints filed under this subchapter and under the Rehabilitation Act of 1973 are dealt with in a manner that avoids duplication of effort and prevents imposition of inconsistent or conflicting standards for the same requirements under this subchapter and the Rehabilitation Act of 1973. The Commission, the Attorney General, and the Office of Federal Contract Compliance Programs shall establish such coordinating mechanisms (similar to provisions contained in the joint regulations promulgated by the Commission and the Attorney General at part 42 of title 28 and part 1691 of title 29, Code of Federal Regulations, and the Memorandum of Understanding between the Commission and the Office of Federal Contract Compliance Programs dated January 16, 1981 (46 Fed.Reg. 7435, January 23, 1981)) in regulations implementing this subchapter and Rehabilitation Act of 1973 not later than 18 months after July 26, 1990.

TITLE V—MISCELLANEOUS PROVISIONS

Sec. 501 [42 U.S.C. § 12201]. Construction

(a) In General

Except as provided in this chapter, nothing in this chapter shall be construed to apply a lesser standard than the standards applied under title V of the Rehabilitation Act of 1973 (29 U.S.C. § 790 et seq.) or the regulations issued by Federal agencies pursuant to such title.

(b) Relationship to other laws

Nothing in this chapter shall be construed to invalidate or limit the remedies, rights, and procedures of any Federal law or law of any State or political subdivision of any State or jurisdiction that provides greater or equal protection for the rights of individuals with disabilities than are afforded by this chapter. Nothing in this chapter shall be construed to preclude the prohibition of, or the imposition of restrictions on, smoking in places of employment covered by subchapter I, in transportation covered by subchapter II or III of this chapter, or in places of public accommodation covered by subchapter III of this chapter.

(c) Insurance

Subchapters I through IV of this chapter and title II of this Act shall not be construed to prohibit or restrict—

(1) an insurer, hospital or medical service company, health maintenance organization, or any agent, or entity that administers benefit plans, or similar organizations from underwriting risks, classifying risks, or administering such risks that are based on or not inconsistent with State law; or

(2) a person or organization covered by this chapter from establishing, sponsoring, observing or administering the terms of bona fide benefit plan that are based on underwriting risks, classifying risks, or administering such risks that are based on or not inconsistent with State law; or

(3) a person or organization covered by this chapter from establishing, sponsoring, observing or administering the terms of a bona fide benefit plan that is not subject to State laws that regulate insurance.

Paragraphs (1), (2), and (3) shall not be used as a subterfuge to evade the purposes of subchapters I and III of this chapter.

(d) Accommodations and services

Nothing in this chapter shall be construed to require an individual with a disability to accept an accommodation, aid, service, opportunity, or benefit which such individual chooses not to accept.

(e) Benefits under State worker's compensation laws[8]

Nothing in this chapter alters the standards for determining eligibility for benefits under State worker's compensation laws or under State and Federal disability benefit programs.

* * *

8. Sections (e), (g), and (h), which are printed in italics, were added by § 6(a) of the ADA Amendments Act of 2008, Pub. L.No. 110–325, 122 Stat. 3553 (2008).

(g) Claims of no disability

Nothing in this chapter shall provide the basis for a claim by an individual without a disability that the individual was subject to discrimination because of the individual's lack of disability.

(h) Reasonable accommodations and modifications

A covered entity under subchapter I of this chapter, a public entity under subchapter II of this chapter, and any person who owns, leases (or leases to), or operates a place of public accommodation under subchapter III of this chapter, need not provide a reasonable accommodation or a reasonable modification to policies, practices, or procedures to an individual who meets the definition of disability in section 12102(1) of this title solely under subparagraph (C) of such section.

Sec. 502 [42 U.S.C. § 12202]. State immunity

A State shall not be immune under the eleventh amendment to the Constitution of the United States from an action in Federal or State court of competent jurisdiction for a violation of this chapter. In any action against a State for a violation of the requirements of this chapter, remedies (including remedies both at law and in equity) are available for such a violation to the same extent as such remedies are available for such a violation in an action against any public or private entity other than a State.

Sec. 503 [42 U.S.C. § 12203]. Prohibition against retaliation and coercion.

(a) Retaliation

No person shall discriminate against any individual because such individual has opposed any act or practice made unlawful by this chapter or because such individual made a charge, testified, assisted, or participated in any manner in an investigation, proceeding, or hearing under this chapter.

(b) Interference, coercion, or intimidation

It shall be unlawful to coerce, intimidate, threaten, or interfere with any individual in the exercise or enjoyment of, or on account of his or her having exercised or enjoyed, or on account of his or her having aided or encouraged any other individual in the exercise or enjoyment of, any right granted or protected by this chapter.

(c) Remedies and procedures

The remedies and procedures available under sections 107, 203, and 308 of this Act [42 U.S.C. §§ 12117, 12133, and 12188] shall be available to aggrieved persons for violations of subsections (a) and (b) of this section, with respect to subchapter I, subchapter II and subchapter III of this chapter, respectively.

* * *

Sec. 505 [42 U.S.C. § 12205]. Attorney's fees

In any action or administrative proceeding commenced pursuant to this chapter, the court or agency, in its discretion, may allow the prevailing party, other than the United States, a reasonable attorney's fee, including litigation expenses, and costs, and the United States shall be liable for the foregoing the same as a private individual.

Sec. 505a [42 U.S.C. § 12205a]. Rule of construction regarding regulatory authority[9]

The authority to issue regulations granted to the Equal Employment Opportunity Commission, the Attorney General, and the Secretary of Transportation under this chapter includes the authority to issue regulations implementing the definitions of disability in section 12102 of this title (including rules of construction) and the definitions in section 12103 of this title, consistent with the ADA Amendments Act of 2008.

* * *

Sec. 508 [42 U.S.C. § 12208]. Transvestites

For the purposes of this chapter, the term "disabled" or "disability" shall not apply to an individual solely because that individual is a transvestite.

Sec. 509 [42 U.S.C. § 12209]. Coverage of Congress and the agencies of the legislative branch

(a) Coverage of the Senate

(1) Commitment to Rule XLII

The Senate reaffirms its commitment to Rule XLII of the Standing Rules of the Senate which provides as follows:

No member, officer, or employee of the Senate shall, with respect to employment by the Senate or any office thereof—

(a) fail or refuse to hire an individual;

(b) discharge an individual; or

(c) otherwise discriminate against an individual with respect to promotion, compensation, or terms, conditions, or privileges of employment on the basis of such individual's race, color, religion, sex, national origin, age, or state of physical handicap.

9. Section 505a, which is printed in italics, was added by § 6(2) of the ADA Amendments Act of 2008, Pub.L.No. 110–325, 122 Stat. 3553 (2008).

(2) Matters other than employment—

(A) In General

The rights and protections under this chapter shall, subject to subparagraph (B), apply with respect to the conduct of the Senate regarding matters other than employment.

(B) Remedies

The Architect of the Capitol shall establish remedies and procedures to be utilized with respect to the rights and protections provided pursuant to subparagraph (A). Such remedies and procedures shall apply exclusively, after approval in accordance with subparagraph (C).

(C) Proposed remedies and procedures

For purposes of subparagraph (B), the Architect of the Capitol shall submit proposed remedies and procedures to the Senate Committee on Rules and Administration. The remedies and procedures shall be effective upon the approval of the Committee on Rules and Administration.

(3) Exercise of rulemaking power

Notwithstanding any other provision of law, enforcement and adjudication of the rights and protections referred to in paragraph (2)(A) shall be within the exclusive jurisdiction of the United States Senate. The provisions of paragraph (1), and (2) are enacted by the Senate as an exercise of the rulemaking power of the Senate, with full recognition of the right of the Senate to change its rules, in the same manner, and to the same extent, as in the case of any other rule of the Senate.

(b) Coverage of the House of Representatives

(1) In General

Notwithstanding any other provision of this chapter or of law, the purposes of this chapter shall, subject to paragraphs (2) and (3), apply in their entirety to the House of Representatives.

(2) Employment in the House

(A) Application

The rights and protections under this chapter shall, subject to subparagraph (B), apply with respect to any employee in an employment position in the House of Representatives and any employing authority of the House of Representatives.

(B) Administration

(i) In general

In the administration of this paragraph, the remedies and procedures made applicable pursuant to the resolution described in clause (ii) shall apply exclusively.

(ii) Resolution

The resolution referred to in clause (i) is House Resolution 15 of the One Hundred First Congress, as agreed to January 3,

1989, or any other provision that continues in effect the provisions of, or is a successor to, the Fair Employment Practices Resolution (House Resolution 558 of the One Hundredth Congress, as agreed to October 4, 1988).

(C) Exercise of rulemaking power

The provisions of subparagraph (B) are enacted by the House of Representatives as an exercise of the rulemaking power of the House of Representatives, with full recognition of the right of the House to change its rules, in the same manner, and to the same extent as in the case of any other rule of the House.

(3) Matters other than employment

(A) In general

The rights and protections under this chapter shall, subject to subparagraph (B), apply with respect to the conduct of the House of Representatives regarding matters other than employment.

(B) Remedies

The Architect of the Capitol shall establish remedies and procedures to be utilized with respect to the rights and protections provided pursuant to subparagraph (A). Such remedies and procedures shall apply exclusively, after approval in accordance with subparagraph (C).

(C) Approval

For purposes of subparagraph (B), the Architect of the Capitol shall submit proposed remedies and procedures to the Speaker of the House of Representatives. The remedies and procedures shall be effective upon the approval of the Speaker, after consultation with the House Office Building Commission.

(c) Instrumentalities of Congress

(1) In general

The rights and protections under this chapter shall, subject to paragraph (2), apply with respect to the conduct of each instrumentality of the Congress.

(2) Establishment of remedies and procedures by instrumentalities

The chief official of each instrumentality of the Congress shall establish remedies and procedures to be utilized with respect to the rights and protections provided pursuant to paragraph (1). Such remedies and procedures shall apply exclusively, except for the employees who are defined as Senate employees in section 120(c)(1) of this title.

(3) Report to Congress

The chief official of each instrumentality of the Congress shall, after establishing remedies and procedures for purposes of paragraph (2), submit to the Congress a report describing the remedies and procedures.

(4) Definition of instrumentalities

For purposes of this section, instrumentalities of the Congress include the following: the Architect of the Capitol, the Congressional Budget Office, the General Accounting Office, the Government Printing Office, and the Library of Congress, the Office of Technology Assessment, and the United States Botanic Garden.

(5) Construction

Nothing in this section shall alter the enforcement procedures for individuals with disabilities provided in the General Accounting Office Personnel Act 1980 and regulations promulgated pursuant to that Act.

Sec. 510 [42 U.S.C. § 12210]. Illegal use of drugs

(a) In general

For purposes of this chapter, the term "individual with a disability" does not include an individual who is currently engaging in the illegal use of drugs, when the covered entity acts on the basis of such use.

(b) Rules of construction

Nothing in subsection (a) of this section shall be construed to exclude as an individual with a disability an individual who—

(1) has successfully completed a supervised drug rehabilitation program and is no longer engaging in the illegal use of drugs, or has otherwise been rehabilitated successfully and is no longer engaging in such use;

(2) is participating in a supervised rehabilitation program and is no longer engaging in such use; or

(3) is erroneously regarded as engaging in such use, but is not engaging in such use;

except that it shall not be a violation of this chapter for a covered entity to adopt or administer reasonable policies or procedures, including but not limited to drug testing, designed to ensure that an individual described in paragraph (1) or (2) is no longer engaging in the illegal use of drugs; however, nothing in this section shall be construed to encourage, prohibit, restrict, or authorize the conducting of testing for the illegal use of drugs.

(c) Health and other services

Notwithstanding subsection (a) and section 511(b)(3) [42 U.S.C. § 12211(b)(3)], an individual shall not be denied health services, or services provided in connection with drug rehabilitation, on the basis of the current illegal use of drugs if the individual is otherwise entitled to such services.

(d) "Illegal use of drugs" defined

(1) In general

The term "illegal use of drugs" means the use of drugs, the possession or distribution of which is unlawful under the Controlled

Substances Act [21 § U.S.C. 801 et seq.]. Such term does not include the use of a drug taken under supervision by a licensed health care professional, or other uses authorized by the Controlled Substances Act or other provisions of Federal law.

(2) Drugs

The term "drug" means a controlled substance, as defined in schedules I through V of section 202 of the Controlled Substances Act [21 U.S.C. § 812].

Sec. 511 [42 U.S.C. § 12211]. Definitions

(a) Homosexuality and bisexuality

For purposes of the definition of "disability" in section 3(2) [42 U.S.C. § 12101(2)], homosexuality and bisexuality are not impairments and as such are not disabilities under this chapter.

(b) Certain conditions

Under this chapter, the term "disability" shall not include—

(1) transvestism, transsexualism, pedophilia, exhibitionism, voyeurism, gender identity disorders not resulting from physical impairments, or other sexual behavior disorders;

(2) compulsive gambling, kleptomania, or pyromania; or

(3) psychoactive substance use disorders resulting from current illegal use of drugs.

Sec. 513 [42 U.S.C. § 12212]. Alternative means of dispute resolution

Where appropriate and to the extent authorized by law, the use of alternative means of dispute resolution, including settlement negotiations, conciliation, facilitation, mediation, factfinding, minitrials, and arbitration, is encouraged to resolve disputes arising under this Act.

Sec. 514 [42 U.S.C. § 12213]. Severability

Should any provision in this chapter be found to be unconstitutional by a court of law, such provision shall be severed from the remainder of the chapter, and such action shall not affect the enforceability of the remaining provisions of the chapter.

ADA AMENDMENTS ACT OF 2008
Pub.L.No. 110–325, 122 Stat. 3553 (2008)

Sec. 1. Short Title

This Act may be cited as the "ADA Amendments Act of 2008".

Sec. 2. Findings and Purposes

(a) Findings

Congress finds that—

(1) in enacting the Americans with Disabilities Act of 1990 (ADA), Congress intended that the Act "provide a clear and comprehensive national mandate for the elimination of discrimination against individuals with disabilities" and provide broad coverage;

(2) in enacting the ADA, Congress recognized that physical and mental disabilities in no way diminish a person's right to fully participate in all aspects of society, but that people with physical or mental disabilities are frequently precluded from doing so because of prejudice, antiquated attitudes, or the failure to remove societal and institutional barriers;

(3) while Congress expected that the definition of disability under the ADA would be interpreted consistently with how courts had applied the definition of a handicapped individual under the Rehabilitation Act of 1973, that expectation has not been fulfilled;

(4) the holdings of the Supreme Court in *Sutton v. United Air Lines, Inc.*, 527 U.S. 471 (1999) and its companion cases have narrowed the broad scope of protection intended to be afforded by the ADA, thus eliminating protection for many individuals whom Congress intended to protect;

(5) the holding of the Supreme Court in *Toyota Motor Manufacturing, Kentucky, Inc. v. Williams*, 534 U.S. 184 (2002) further narrowed the broad scope of protection intended to be afforded by the ADA;

(6) as a result of these Supreme Court cases, lower courts have incorrectly found in individual cases that people with a range of substantially limiting impairments are not people with disabilities;

(7) in particular, the Supreme Court, in the case of *Toyota Motor Manufacturing, Kentucky, Inc. v. Williams*, 534 U.S. 184 (2002), interpreted the term "substantially limits" to require a greater degree of limitation than was intended by Congress; and

(8) Congress finds that the current Equal Employment Opportunity Commission ADA regulations defining the term "substantially limits" as "significantly restricted" are inconsistent with congressional intent, by expressing too high a standard.

(b) Purposes

The purposes of this Act are—

(1) to carry out the ADA's objectives of providing "a clear and comprehensive national mandate for the elimination of discrimination" and "clear, strong, consistent, enforceable standards addressing discrimination" by reinstating a broad scope of protection to be available under the ADA;

(2) to reject the requirement enunciated by the Supreme Court in *Sutton v. United Air Lines, Inc.*, 527 U.S. 471 (1999) and its companion cases that whether an impairment substantially limits a major life activity is to be determined with reference to the ameliorative effects of mitigating measures;

(3) to reject the Supreme Court's reasoning in *Sutton v. United Air Lines, Inc.*, 527 U.S. 471 (1999) with regard to coverage under the third prong of the definition of disability and to reinstate the reasoning of the Supreme Court in *School Board of Nassau County v. Arline*, 480 U.S. 273 (1987) which set forth a broad view of the third prong of the definition of handicap under the Rehabilitation Act of 1973;

(4) to reject the standards enunciated by the Supreme Court in *Toyota Motor Manufacturing, Kentucky, Inc. v. Williams*, 534 U.S. 184 (2002), that the terms "substantially" and "major" in the definition of disability under the ADA "need to be interpreted strictly to create a demanding standard for qualifying as disabled," and that to be substantially limited in performing a major life activity under the ADA "an individual must have an impairment that prevents or severely restricts the individual from doing activities that are of central importance to most people's daily lives";

(5) to convey congressional intent that the standard created by the Supreme Court in the case of *Toyota Motor Manufacturing, Kentucky, Inc. v. Williams*, 534 U.S. 184 (2002) for "substantially limits", and applied by lower courts in numerous decisions, has created an inappropriately high level of limitation necessary to obtain coverage under the ADA, to convey that it is the intent of Congress that the primary object of attention in cases brought under the ADA should be whether entities covered under the ADA have complied with their obligations, and to convey that the question of whether an individual's impairment is a disability under the ADA should not demand extensive analysis; and

(6) to express Congress' expectation that the Equal Employment Opportunity Commission will revise that portion of its current regulations that defines the term "substantially limits" as "significantly restricted" to be consistent with this Act, including the amendments made by this Act.

* * *

Sec. 8. Effective Date

This Act and the amendments made by this Act shall become effective on January 1, 2009.

GENETIC INFORMATION NONDISCRIMINATION ACT OF 2008 Pub.L.No. 110–233, 122 Stat. 881 (2008) (Codified at 42 U.S.C. § 2000ff)[1]

Sec. 2 [42 U.S.C. § 2000ff Note]. Findings

Congress makes the following findings:

(1) Deciphering the sequence of the human genome and other advances in genetics open major new opportunities for medical progress. New knowledge about the genetic basis of illness will allow for earlier detection of illnesses, often before symptoms have begun. Genetic testing can allow individuals to take steps to reduce the likelihood that they will contract a particular disorder. New knowledge about genetics may allow for the development of better therapies that are more effective against disease or have fewer side effects than current treatments. These advances give rise to the potential misuse of genetic information to discriminate in health insurance and employment.

(2) The early science of genetics became the basis of State laws that provided for the sterilization of persons having presumed genetic "defects" such as mental retardation, mental disease, epilepsy, blindness, and hearing loss, among other conditions. The first sterilization law was enacted in the State of Indiana in 1907. By 1981, a majority of States adopted sterilization laws to "correct" apparent genetic traits or tendencies. Many of these State laws have since been repealed, and many have been modified to include essential constitutional requirements of due process and equal protection. However, the current explosion in the science of genetics, and the history of sterilization laws by the States based on early genetic science, compels Congressional action in this area.

(3) Although genes are facially neutral markers, many genetic conditions and disorders are associated with particular racial and ethnic groups and gender. Because some genetic traits are most prevalent in particular groups, members of a particular group may be stigmatized or discriminated against as a result of that genetic information. This form of discrimination was evident in the 1970s, which saw the advent of programs to screen and identify carriers of sickle cell anemia, a disease which afflicts African–Americans. Once again, State legislatures began to enact discriminatory laws in the area, and in the early 1970s began mandating genetic screening of all African Americans for sickle cell anemia, leading to discrimination and unnecessary fear. To alleviate some of this stigma, Congress in 1972 passed the National Sickle Cell

1. Section 213 of the Genetic Information Nondiscrimination Act, Pub.L.No. 110–233, 122 Stat. 881 (2008) provides: "This title takes effect on the date that is 18 months after the date of enactment of this Act."

Anemia Control Act, which withholds Federal funding from States unless sickle cell testing is voluntary.

(4) Congress has been informed of examples of genetic discrimination in the workplace. These include the use of pre-employment genetic screening at Lawrence Berkeley Laboratory, which led to a court decision in favor of the employees in that case *Norman–Bloodsaw v. Lawrence Berkeley Laboratory* (135 F.3d 1260, 1269 (9th Cir. 1998)). Congress clearly has a compelling public interest in relieving the fear of discrimination and in prohibiting its actual practice in employment and health insurance.

(5) Federal law addressing genetic discrimination in health insurance and employment is incomplete in both the scope and depth of its protections. Moreover, while many States have enacted some type of genetic non-discrimination law, these laws vary widely with respect to their approach, application, and level of protection. Congress has collected substantial evidence that the American public and the medical community find the existing patchwork of State and Federal laws to be confusing and inadequate to protect them from discrimination. Therefore Federal legislation establishing a national and uniform basic standard is necessary to fully protect the public from discrimination and allay their concerns about the potential for discrimination, thereby allowing individuals to take advantage of genetic testing, technologies, research, and new therapies.

* * *

TITLE II—PROHIBITING EMPLOYMENT DISCRIMINATION ON THE BASIS OF GENETIC INFORMATION

Sec. 201 [42 U.S.C. § 2000ff]. Definitions

In this chapter

* * *

(3) Family member

The term "family member" means, with respect to an individual—

(A) a dependent (as such term is used for purposes of section 1181(f)(2) of Title 29 of such individual), and

(B) any other individual who is a first-degree, second-degree, third-degree, or fourth-degree relative of such individual or of an individual described in subparagraph (A).

(4) Genetic information

(A) In general

The term "genetic information" means, with respect to any individual, information about—

(i) such individual's genetic tests,

(ii) the genetic tests of family members of such individual, and

(iii) the manifestation of a disease or disorder in family members of such individual.

(B) Inclusion of genetic services and participation in genetic research

Such term includes, with respect to any individual, any request for, or receipt of, genetic services, or participation in clinical research which includes genetic services, by such individual or any family member of such individual.

(C) Exclusions

The term "genetic information" shall not include information about the sex or age of any individual.

(5) Genetic monitoring

The term "genetic monitoring" means the periodic examination of employees to evaluate acquired modifications to their genetic material, such as chromosomal damage or evidence of increased occurrence of mutations, that may have developed in the course of employment due to exposure to toxic substances in the workplace, in order to identify, evaluate, and respond to the effects of or control adverse environmental exposures in the workplace.

(6) Genetic services

The term "genetic services" means—

(A) a genetic test;

(B) genetic counseling (including obtaining, interpreting, or assessing genetic information); or

(C) genetic education.

(7) Genetic test

(A) In general

The term "genetic test" means an analysis of human DNA, RNA, chromosomes, proteins, or metabolites, that detects genotypes, mutations, or chromosomal changes.

(B) Exceptions

The term "genetic test" does not mean an analysis of proteins or metabolites that does not detect genotypes, mutations, or chromosomal changes.

Sec. 202 [42 U.S.C. § 2000ff–1]. Employer practices[2]

(a) Discrimination based on genetic information

It shall be an unlawful employment practice for an employer—

2. The Genetic Information Nondiscrimination Act of 2008, in sections omitted here, also covers employment agency practices (§ 203), labor organization practices (§ 204), and training programs (§ 205). Remedies and enforcement are covered in § 207, which essentially tracks the enforcement procedures and remedies under Title VII of the Civil Rights Act of 1964.

(1) to fail or refuse to hire, or to discharge, any employee, or otherwise to discriminate against any employee with respect to the compensation, terms, conditions, or privileges of employment of the employee, because of genetic information with respect to the employee; or

(2) to limit, segregate, or classify the employees of the employer in any way that would deprive or tend to deprive any employee of employment opportunities or otherwise adversely affect the status of the employee as an employee, because of genetic information with respect to the employee.

(b) Acquisition of genetic information

It shall be an unlawful employment practice for an employer to request, require, or purchase genetic information with respect to an employee or a family member of the employee except—

(1) where an employer inadvertently requests or requires family medical history of the employee or family member of the employee;

(2) where—

(A) health or genetic services are offered by the employer, including such services offered as part of a wellness program;

(B) the employee provides prior, knowing, voluntary, and written authorization;

(C) only the employee (or family member if the family member is receiving genetic services) and the licensed health care professional or board certified genetic counselor involved in providing such services receive individually identifiable information concerning the results of such services; and

(D) any individually identifiable genetic information provided under subparagraph (C) in connection with the services provided under subparagraph (A) is only available for purposes of such services and shall not be disclosed to the employer except in aggregate terms that do not disclose the identity of specific employees;

(3) where an employer requests or requires family medical history from the employee to comply with the certification provisions of section 2613 of Title 29 or such requirements under State family and medical leave laws;

(4) where an employer purchases documents that are commercially and publicly available (including newspapers, magazines, periodicals, and books, but not including medical databases or court records) that include family medical history;

(5) where the information involved is to be used for genetic monitoring of the biological effects of toxic substances in the workplace, but only if—

(A) the employer provides written notice of the genetic monitoring to the employee;

(B)(i) the employee provides prior, knowing, voluntary, and written authorization; or

(ii) the genetic monitoring is required by Federal or State law;

(C) the employee is informed of individual monitoring results;

(D) the monitoring is in compliance with—

(i) any Federal genetic monitoring regulations, including any such regulations that may be promulgated by the Secretary of Labor pursuant to the Occupational Safety and Health Act of 1970 (29 U.S.C. 651 et seq.), the Federal Mine Safety and Health Act of 1977 (30 U.S.C. 801 et seq.), or the Atomic Energy Act of 1954 (42 U.S.C. 2011 et seq.); or

(ii) State genetic monitoring regulations, in the case of a State that is implementing genetic monitoring regulations under the authority of the Occupational Safety and Health Act of 1970 (29 U.S.C. 651 et seq.); and

(E) the employer, excluding any licensed health care professional or board certified genetic counselor that is involved in the genetic monitoring program, receives the results of the monitoring only in aggregate terms that do not disclose the identity of specific employees; or

(6) where the employer conducts DNA analysis for law enforcement purposes as a forensic laboratory or for purposes of human remains identification, and requests or requires genetic information of such employer's employees, but only to the extent that such genetic information is used for analysis of DNA identification markers for quality control to detect sample contamination.

(c) Preservation of protections

In the case of information to which any of paragraphs (1) through (6) of subsection (b) applies, such information may not be used in violation of paragraph (1) or (2) of subsection (a) or treated or disclosed in a manner that violates section 2000ff–5 of this title.

Sec. 206 [§ 2000ff–5]. Confidentiality of genetic information

(a) Treatment of information as part of confidential medical record

If an employer, employment agency, labor organization, or joint labor-management committee possesses genetic information about an employee or member, such information shall be maintained on separate forms and in separate medical files and be treated as a confidential medical record of the employee or member. An employer, employment agency, labor organization, or joint labor-management committee shall be considered to be in compliance with the maintenance of information requirements of this subsection with respect to genetic information subject to this subsection that is maintained with and treated as a confidential medical record under section 12112(d)(3)(B) of this title.

(b) Limitation on disclosure

An employer, employment agency, labor organization, or joint labor-management committee shall not disclose genetic information concerning an employee or member except—

(1) to the employee or member of a labor organization (or family member if the family member is receiving the genetic services) at the written request of the employee or member of such organization;

(2) to an occupational or other health researcher if the research is conducted in compliance with the regulations and protections provided for under part 46 of title 45, Code of Federal Regulations;

(3) in response to an order of a court, except that—

(A) the employer, employment agency, labor organization, or joint labor-management committee may disclose only the genetic information expressly authorized by such order; and

(B) if the court order was secured without the knowledge of the employee or member to whom the information refers, the employer, employment agency, labor organization, or joint labor-management committee shall inform the employee or member of the court order and any genetic information that was disclosed pursuant to such order;

(4) to government officials who are investigating compliance with this chapter if the information is relevant to the investigation;

(5) to the extent that such disclosure is made in connection with the employee's compliance with the certification provisions of section 2613 of Title 29 or such requirements under State family and medical leave laws; or

(6) to a Federal, State, or local public health agency only with regard to information that is described in section 2000ff(4)(A)(iii) of this title and that concerns a contagious disease that presents an imminent hazard of death or life-threatening illness, and that the employee whose family member or family members is or are the subject of a disclosure under this paragraph is notified of such disclosure.

* * *

Sec. 208 [42 U.S.C. § 2000ff–7]. Disparate impact

(a) General rule

Notwithstanding any other provision of this Act, "disparate impact", as that term is used in section 2000e–2(k) of this title, on the basis of genetic information does not establish a cause of action under this Act.

* * *

Sec. 210 [42 U.S.C. § 2000ff–9]. Medical information that is not genetic information

An employer, employment agency, labor organization, or joint labor-management committee shall not be considered to be in violation of this chapter based on the use, acquisition, or disclosure of medical information that is not genetic information about a manifested disease, disorder, or pathological condition of an employee or member, including a manifested disease, disorder, or pathological condition that has or may have a genetic basis.

FAMILY AND MEDICAL LEAVE ACT OF 1993
29 U.S.C. §§ 2601–2619, 2651–2654

Sec. 2 [29 U.S.C. § 2601]. Findings and purposes

(a) Findings

Congress finds that—

(1) the number of single-parent households and two-parent households in which the single parent or both parents work is increasing significantly;

(2) it is important for the development of children and the family unit that fathers and mothers be able to participate in early childrearing and the care of family members who have serious health conditions;

(3) the lack of employment policies to accommodate working parents can force individuals to choose between job security and parenting;

(4) there is inadequate job security for employees who have serious health conditions that prevent them from working for temporary periods;

(5) due to the nature of the roles of men and women in our society, the primary responsibility for family caretaking often falls on women, and such responsibility affects the working lives of women more than it affects the working lives of men; and

(6) employment standards that apply to one gender only have serious potential for encouraging employers to discriminate against employees and applicants for employment who are of that gender.

(b) Purposes

It is the purpose of this Act—

(1) to balance the demands of the workplace with the needs of families, to promote the stability and economic security of families, and to promote national interests in preserving family integrity;

(2) to entitle employees to take reasonable leave for medical reasons, for the birth or adoption of a child, and for the care of a child, spouse, or parent who has a serious health condition;

(3) to accomplish the purposes described in paragraphs (1)and (2) in a manner that accommodates the legitimate interests of employers;

(4) to accomplish the purposes described in paragraphs (1) and (2) in a manner that, consistent with the Equal Protection Clause of the Fourteenth Amendment, minimizes the potential for employment discrimination on the basis of sex by ensuring generally that leave is

available for eligible medical reasons (including maternity-related disability) and for compelling family reasons, on a gender-neutral basis; and

(5) to promote the goal of equal employment opportunity for women and men, pursuant to such clause.

TITLE I—GENERAL LEAVE REQUIREMENT

Sec. 101 [29 U.S.C. § 2611]. Definitions

As used in this title:

(1) Commerce

The terms "commerce" and "industry or activity affecting commerce" means any activity, business, or industry in commerce or in which a labor dispute would hinder or obstruct commerce or the free flow of commerce, and include "commerce" and any "industry affecting commerce," as defined in paragraphs (1) and (3) of section 501 of the Labor Management Relations Act, 1947 [29 U.S.C. §§ 142(1) and (3)].

(2) Eligible employee

(A) In general

The term "eligible employee" means an employee who has been employed—

(i) for at least 12 months by the employer with respect to whom leave is requested under section 102; and

(ii) for at least 1,250 hours of service with such employer during the previous 12–month period.

(B) Exclusions

The term "eligible employee" does not include—

(i) any Federal officer or employee covered under subchapter V of chapter 63 of title 5, United States Code (as added by title II of this Act); or

(ii) any employee of an employer who is employed at a worksite at which such employer employs less than 50 employees if the total number of employees employed by that employer within 75 miles of that worksite is less than 50.

(C) Determination

For purposes of determining whether an employee meets the hours of service requirement specified in subparagraph (A)(ii), the legal standards established under section 7 of the Fair Labor Standards Act of 1938 [29 U.S.C. § 207] shall apply.

(3) Employ; employee; state

The terms "employ", "employee", and "State" have the same meanings given such terms in subsections (c), (e), and (g) of section 3 of the Fair Labor Standards Act of 1938 [29 U.S.C. §§ 203(c), (e), and (g)].

(4) Employer

(A) In general

The term "employer"—

(i) means any person engaged in commerce or in any industry or activity affecting commerce who employs 50 or more employees for each working day during each of 20 or more calendar workweeks in the current or preceding calendar year;

(ii) includes—

(I) any person who acts, directly or indirectly, in the interest of an employer to any of the employees of such employer; and interest of an employer to any of the employees of such employer; and

(II) any successor in interest of an employer; and

(iii) includes any "public agency," as defined in section 3(x) of the Fair Labor Standards Act of 1938 [29 U.S.C. § 203(x)].

(B) Public agency

For purposes of subparagraph (A)(iii), a public agency shall be considered to be a person engaged in commerce or in an industry or activity affecting commerce.

(5) Employment benefits

The term "employment benefits" means all benefits provided or made available to employees by an employer, including group life insurance, health insurance, disability insurance, sick leave, annual leave, educational benefits, and pensions, regardless of whether such benefits are provided by a practice or written policy of an employer or through an "employee benefit plan", as defined in section 3(3) of the Employee Retirement Income Security Act of 1974 [29 U.S.C. § 1002(3)].

(6) Health care provider

The term "health care provider" means—

(A) a doctor of medicine or osteopathy who is authorized to practice medicine or surgery (as appropriate) by the State in which the doctor practices; or

(B) any other person determined by the Secretary to be capable of providing health care services.

(7) Parent

The term "parent" means the biological parent of an employee or an individual who stood in loco parentis to an employee when the employee was a son or daughter.

(8) Person

The Term "person" has the same meaning given such term in section 3(a) of the Fair Labor Standards Act of 1938 [29 U.S.C. § 203(a)].

(9) Reduced leave schedule

The term "reduced leave schedule" means a leave schedule that reduces the usual number of hours per workweek, or hours per workday, of an employee.

(10) Secretary

The term "Secretary" means the Secretary of Labor.

(11) Serious health condition

The term "serious health condition" means an illness, injury, impairment, or physical or mental condition that involves—

(A) inpatient care in a hospital, hospice, or residential medical care facility; or

(B) continuing treatment by a health care provider.

(12) Son or daughter

The term "son or daughter" means a biological, adopted, or foster child, a stepchild, a legal ward, or a child of a person standing in loco parentis, who is—

(A) under 18 years of age; or

(B) 18 years of age or older and incapable of self-care because of a mental or physical disability.

(13) Spouse

The term "spouse" means a husband or wife, as the case may be.

Sec. 102 [29 U.S.C. § 2612]. Leave requirement

(a) In general

(1) Entitlement to leave

Subject to section 103, an eligible employee shall be entitled to a total of 12 workweeks of leave during any 12–month period for one or more of the following:

(A) Because of the birth of a son or daughter of the employee and in order to care for such son or daughter.

(B) Because of the placement of a son or daughter with the employee for adoption or foster care.

(C) In order to care for the spouse, or a son, daughter, or parent, of the employee, if such spouse, son, daughter, or parent has a serious health condition.

(D) Because of a serious health condition that makes the employee unable to perform the functions of the position of such employee.

(2) Expiration of entitlement

The entitlement to leave under subparagraphs (A) and (B) of paragraph (1) for a birth or placement of a son or daughter shall expire at the end of the 12-month period beginning on the date of such birth or placement.

(b) Leave taken intermittently or on a reduced leave schedule

(1) In general

Leave under subparagraph (A) or (B) of subsection (a)(1) shall not be taken by an employee intermittently or on a reduced leave schedule unless the employee and the employer of the employee agree otherwise. Subject to paragraph (2), subsection (e)(2), and section 103(b)(5), leave under subparagraph (C) or (D) of subsection (a)(1) may be taken intermittently or on a reduced leave schedule when medically necessary. The taking of leave intermittently or on a reduced leave schedule pursuant to this paragraph shall not result in a reduction in the total amount of leave to which the employee is entitled under subsection (a) beyond the amount of leave actually taken.

(2) Alternative position

If an employee requests intermittent leave, or leave on a reduced leave schedule, under subparagraph (C) or (D) of subsection (a)(1), that is foreseeable based on planned medical treatment, the employer may require such employee to transfer temporarily to an available alternative position offered by the employer for which the employee is qualified and that—

(A) has equivalent pay and benefits; and

(B) better accommodates recurring periods of leave than the regular employment position of the employee.

(c) Unpaid leave permitted

Except as provided in subsection (d), leave granted under subsection (a) may consist of unpaid leave. Where an employee is otherwise exempt under regulations issued by the Secretary pursuant to section 13(a)(1) of the Fair Labor Standards Act of 1938 [29 U.S.C. § 213(a)(1)], the compliance of an employer with this title by providing unpaid leave shall not affect the exempt status of the employee under such section.

(d) Relationship to paid leave

(1) Unpaid leave

If an employer provides paid leave for fewer than 12 workweeks, the additional weeks of leave necessary to attain the 12 workweeks of leave required under this title may be provided without compensation.

(2) Substitution of paid leave

(A) In general

An eligible employee may elect, or an employer may require the employee, to substitute any of the accrued paid vacation leave, personal leave, or family leave of the employee for leave provided under subparagraph (A), (B), or (C) of subsection (a)(1) for any part of the 12–week period of such leave under such subsection.

(B) Serious health condition

An eligible employee may elect, or an employer may require the employee, to substitute any of the accrued paid vacation leave, personal leave, or medical or sick leave of the employee for leave provided under subparagraph (C) or (D) of subsection (a)(1) for any part of the 12–week period of such leave under such subsection, except that nothing in this title shall require an employer to provide paid sick leave or paid medical leave in any situation in which such employer would not normally provide any such paid leave.

(e) Foreseeable leave

(1) Requirement of notice

In any case in which the necessity for leave under subparagraph (A) or (B) of subsection (a)(1) is foreseeable based on an expected birth or placement, the employee shall provide the employer with not less than 30 days' notice, before the date the leave is to begin, of the employee's intention to take leave under such subparagraph, except that if the date of the birth or placement requires leave to begin in less than 30 days, the employee shall provide such notice as is practicable.

(2) Duties of employee

In any case in which the necessity for leave under subparagraph (C) or (D) of subsection (a)(1) is foreseeable based on planned medical treatment, the employee—

(A) shall make a reasonable effort to schedule the treatment so as not to disrupt unduly the operations of the employer, subject to the approval of the health care provider of the employee or the health care provider of the son, daughter, spouse, or parent of the employee, as appropriate; and

(B) shall provide the employer with not less than 30 days' notice, before the date the leave is to begin, of the employee's intention to take leave under such subparagraph, except that if the date of the treatment requires leave to begin in less than 30 days, the employee shall provide such notice as is practicable.

(f) Spouses employed by the same employer

In any case in which a husband and wife entitled to leave under subsection (a) are employed by the same employer, the aggregate number of workweeks of leave to which both may be entitled may be limited to 12 workweeks during any 12–month period, if such leave is taken—

(1) under subparagraph (A) or (B) of subsection (a)(1); or

(2) to care for a sick parent under subparagraph (C) of such subsection.

Sec. 103 [29 U.S.C. § 2613]. Certification

(a) In general

An employer may require that a request for leave under subparagraph (C) or (D) of section 102(a)(1) be supported by a certification issued by the health care provider of the eligible employee or of the son, daughter, spouse, or parent of the employee, as appropriate. The employee shall provide, in a timely manner, a copy of such certification to the employer.

(b) Sufficient certification

Certification provided under subsection (a) shall be sufficient if it states—

(1) the date on which the serious health condition commenced;

(2) the probable duration of the condition;

(3) the appropriate medical facts within the knowledge of the health care provider regarding the condition;

(4)(A) for purposes of leave under section 102(a)(1)(C), a statement that the eligible employee is needed to care for the son, daughter, spouse, or parent and an estimate of the amount of time that such employee is needed to care for the son, daughter, spouse, or parent; and

(B) for purposes of leave under section 102(a)(1)(D), a statement that the employee is unable to perform the functions of the position of the employee;

(5) in the case of certification for intermittent leave, or leave on a reduced leave schedule, for planned medical treatment, the dates on which such treatment is expected to be given and the duration of such treatment;

(6) in the case of certification for intermittent leave, or leave on a reduced leave schedule, under section 102(a)(1)(D), a statement of the medical necessity for the intermittent leave or leave on a reduced leave schedule, and the expected duration of the intermittent leave or reduced leave schedule; and

(7) in the case of certification for intermittent leave, or leave on a reduced leave schedule, under section 102(a)(1)(C), a statement that the employee's intermittent leave or leave on a reduced leave schedule is necessary for the care of the son, daughter, parent, or spouse who has a serious health condition, or will assist in their

recovery, and the expected duration and schedule of the intermittent leave or reduced leave schedule.

(c) Second opinion

(1) In general

In any case in which the employer has reason to doubt the validity of the certification provided under subsection (a) for leave under subparagraph (C) or (D) of section 102(a)(1), the employer may require, at the expense of the employer, that the eligible employee obtain the opinion of a second health care provider designated or approved by the employer concerning any information certified under subsection (b) for such leave.

(2) Limitation

A health care provider designated or approved under paragraph (1) shall not be employed on a regular basis by the employer.

(d) Resolution of conflicting opinions

(1) In general

In any case in which the second opinion described in subsection (c) differs from the opinion in the original certification provided under subsection (a), the employer may require, at the expense of the employer, that the employee obtain the opinion of a third health care provider designated or approved jointly by the employer and the employee concerning the information certified under subsection (b).

(2) Finality

The opinion of the third health care provider concerning the information certified under subsection (b) shall be considered to be final and shall be binding on the employer and the employee.

(e) Subsequent recertification

The employer may require that the eligible employee obtain subsequent recertifications on a reasonable basis.

Sec. 104 [29 U.S.C. § 2614]. Employment and benefits protection

(a) Restoration to position

(1) In general

Except as provided in subsection (b), any eligible employee who takes leave under section 102 for the intended purpose of the leave shall be entitled, on return from such leave—

(A) to be restored by the employer to the position of employment held by the employee when the leave commenced; or

(B) to be restored to an equivalent position with equivalent employment benefits, pay, and other terms and conditions of employment.

(2) Loss of benefits

The taking of leave under section 102 shall not result in the loss of any employment benefit accrued prior to the date on which the leave commenced.

(3) Limitations

Nothing in this section shall be construed to entitle any restored employee to—

(A) the accrual of any seniority or employment benefits during any period of leave; or

(B) any right, benefit, or position of employment other than any right, benefit, or position to which the employee would have been entitled had the employee not taken the leave.

(4) Certification

As a condition of restoration under paragraph (1) for an employee who has taken leave under section 102(a)(1)(D), the employer may have a uniformly applied practice or policy that requires each such employee to receive certification from the health care provider of the employee that the employee is able to resume work, except that nothing in this paragraph shall supersede a valid State or local law or a collective bargaining agreement that governs the return to work of such employees.

(5) Construction

Nothing in this subsection shall be construed to prohibit an employer from requiring an employee on leave under section 102 to report periodically to the employer on the status and intention of the employee to return to work.

(b) Exemption concerning certain highly compensated employees

(1) Denial of restoration

An employer may deny restoration under subsection (a) to any eligible employee described in paragraph (2) if—

(A) such denial is necessary to prevent substantial and grievous economic injury to the operations of the employer;

(B) the employer notifies the employee of the intent of the employer to deny restoration on such basis at the time the employer determines that such injury would occur; and

(C) in any case in which the leave has commenced, the employee elects not to return to employment after receiving such notice.

(2) Affected employees

An eligible employee described in paragraph (1) is a salaried eligible employee who is among the highest paid 10 percent of the employees employed by the employer within 75 miles of the facility at which the employee is employed.

(c) Maintenance of health benefits

(1) Coverage

Except as provided in paragraph (2), during any period that an eligible employee takes leave under section 102, the employer shall maintain coverage under any "group health plan" (as defined in section 5000(b)(1) of the Internal Revenue Code of 1986) for the duration of such leave at the level and under the conditions coverage would have been provided if the employee had continued in employment continuously for the duration of such leave.

(2) Failure to return from leave

The employer may recover the premium that the employer paid for maintaining coverage for the employee under such group health plan during any period of unpaid leave under section 102 if—

(A) the employee fails to return from leave under section 102 after the period of leave to which the employee is entitled has expired; and

(B) the employee fails to return to work for a reason other than—

(i) the continuation, recurrence, or onset of a serious health condition that entitles the employee to leave under subparagraph (C) or (D) of section 102(a)(1); or

(ii) other circumstances beyond the control of the employee.

(3) Certification

(A) Issuance

An employer may require that a claim that an employee is unable to return to work because of the continuation, recurrence, or onset of the serious health condition described in paragraph (2)(B)(i) be supported by—

(i) a certification issued by the health care provider of the son, daughter, spouse, or parent of the employee, as appropriate, in the case of an employee unable to return to work because of a condition specified in section 102(a)(1)(C); or

(ii) a certification issued by the health care provider of the eligible employee, in the case of an employee unable to return to work because of a condition specified in section 102(a)(1)(D).

(B) Copy

The employee shall provide, in a timely manner, a copy of such certification to the employer.

(C) Sufficiency of certification

(i) Leave due to serious health condition of employee

The certification described in subparagraph (A)(ii) shall be sufficient if the certification states that a serious health condition prevented the employee from being able to perform the functions of the position of the employee on the date that the leave of the employee expired.

(ii) Leave due to serious health condition of family member

The certification described in subparagraph (A)(i) shall be sufficient if the certification states that the employee is needed to care for the son, daughter, spouse, or parent who has a serious health condition on the date that the leave of the employee expired.

Sec. 105 [29 U.S.C. § 2615]. Prohibited acts

(a) Interference with rights

(1) Exercise of rights

It shall be unlawful for any employer to interfere with, restrain, or deny the exercise of or the attempt to exercise, any right provided under this title.

(2) Discrimination

It shall be unlawful for any employer to discharge or in any other manner discriminate against any individual for opposing any practice made unlawful by this title.

(b) Interference with proceedings or inquiries

It shall be unlawful for any person to discharge or in any other manner discriminate against any individual because such individual—

(1) has filed any charge, or has instituted or caused to be instituted any proceeding, under or related to this title;

(2) has given, or is about to give, any information in connection with any inquiry or proceeding relating to any right provided under this title; or

(3) has testified, or is about to testify, in any inquiry or proceeding relating to any right provided under this title.

Sec. 106 [29 U.S.C. § 2616]. Investigative authority

(a) In general

To ensure compliance with the provisions of this title, or any regulation or order issued under this title, the Secretary shall have, subject to subsection (c), the investigative authority provided under section 11(a) of the Fair Labor Standards Act of 1938 [29 U.S.C. § 211(a)].

(b) Obligation to keep and preserve records

Any employer shall make, keep, and preserve records pertaining to compliance with this title in accordance with section 11(c) of the Fair Labor Standards Act of 1938 [29 U.S.C. § 211(c)] and in accordance with regulations issued by the Secretary.

(c) Required submissions generally limited to an annual basis

The Secretary shall not under the authority of this section require any employer or any plan, fund, or program to submit to the Secretary any books or records more than once during any 12–month period, unless the Secretary has reasonable cause to believe there may exist a violation of this title or any regulation or order issued pursuant to this title, or is investigating a charge pursuant to section 2617(b) of this title.

(d) Subpoena powers

For the purposes of any investigation provided for in this section, the Secretary shall have the subpoena authority provided for under section 9 of the Fair Labor Standards Act of 1938 [29 U.S.C. § 209].

Sec. 107 [29 U.S.C. § 2617]. Enforcement

(a) Civil action by employees

(1) Liability

Any employer who violates section 2615 shall be liable to any eligible employee affected—

(A) for damages equal to—

(i) the amount of—

(I) any wages, salary, employment benefits, or other compensation denied or lost to such employee by reason of the violation; or

(II) in a case in which wages, salary, employment benefits, or other compensation have not been denied or lost to the employee, any actual monetary losses sustained by the employee as a direct result of the violation, such as the cost of providing care, up to a sum equal to 12 weeks of wages or salary for the employee;

(ii) the interest on the amount described in clause (i) calculated at the prevailing rate; and

(iii) an additional amount as liquidated damages equal to the sum of the amount described in clause (i) and the interest described in clause (ii), except that if an employer who has violated section 2615 of this title proves to the satisfaction of the court that the act or omission which violated section 2615 of this title was in good faith and that the employer had reasonable grounds for believing that the act or omission was not a violation of section 2615 of this title, such court may, in the discretion of the court, reduce the amount of the liability to the amount and interest determined under clauses (i) and (ii), respectively; and

(B) for such equitable relief as may be appropriate, including employment, reinstatement, and promotion.

(2) Right of action

An action to recover the damages or equitable relief prescribed in paragraph (1) may be maintained against any employer (including a public agency) in any Federal or State court of competent jurisdiction by any one or more employees for and in behalf of—

(A) the employees; or

(B) the employees and other employees similarly situated.

(3) Fees and costs

The court in such an action shall, in addition to any judgment awarded to the plaintiff, allow a reasonable attorney's fee, reasonable expert witness fees, and other costs of the action to be paid by the defendant.

(4) Limitations

The right provided by paragraph (2) to bring an action by or on behalf of any employee shall terminate—

(A) on the filing of a complaint by the Secretary in an action under subsection (d) in which restraint is sought of any further delay in the payment of the amount described in paragraph (1)(A) to such employee by an employer responsible under paragraph (1) for the payment; or

(B) on the filing of a complaint by the Secretary in an action under subsection (b) in which a recovery is sought of the damages described in paragraph (1)(A) owing to an eligible employee by an employer liable under paragraph (1), unless the action described in subparagraph (A) or (B) is dismissed without prejudice on motion of the Secretary.

(b) Action by the Secretary

(1) Administrative action

The Secretary shall receive, investigate, and attempt to resolve complaints of violations of section 2615 in the same manner that the Secretary receives, investigates, and attempts to resolve complaints of violations of sections 6 and 7 of the Fair Labor Standards Act of 1938 [29 U.S.C. §§ 206 and 207].

(2) Civil action

The Secretary may bring an action in any court of competent jurisdiction to recover the damages described in subsection (a)(1)(A) of this section.

(3) Sums recovered

Any sums recovered by the Secretary pursuant to paragraph (2) shall be held in a special deposit account and shall be paid, on order of the Secretary, directly to each employee affected. Any such sums not paid to an employee because of inability to do so within a period of 3 years shall be deposited into the Treasury of the United States as miscellaneous receipts.

(c) Limitation

(1) In general

Except as provided in paragraph (2), an action may be brought under this section not later than 2 years after the date of the last event constituting the alleged violation for which the action is brought.

(2) Willful violation

In the case of such action brought for a willful violation of section 2615 of this title, such action may be brought within 3 years of the date of the last event constituting the alleged violation for which such action is brought.

(3) Commencement

In determining when an action is commenced by the Secretary under this section for the purposes of this subsection, it shall be considered to be commenced on the date when the complaint is filed.

(d) Action for injunction by Secretary

The district courts of the United States shall have jurisdiction, for cause shown, in an action brought by the Secretary—

(1) to restrain violations of section 2615 of this title, including the restraint of any withholding of payment of wages, salary, employment benefits, or other compensation, plus interest, found by the court to be due to eligible employees; or

(2) to award such other equitable relief as may be appropriate, including employment, reinstatement, and promotion.

(e) Solicitor of Labor

The Solicitor of Labor may appear for and represent the Secretary on any litigation brought under this section.

Sec. 108 [29 U.S.C. § 2618]. Special rules concerning employees of local educational agencies

(a) Application

(1) In general

Except as otherwise provided in this section, the rights (including the rights under section 2614 of this title, which shall extend throughout the period of leave of any employee under this section), remedies, and procedures under this title shall apply to—

(A) any "local educational agency" (as defined in section 1471(12) of the Elementary and Secondary Education Act of 1965 [20 U.S.C. § 2891(12)]) and an eligible employee of the agency; and

(B) any private elementary or secondary school and an eligible employee of the school.

(2) Definitions

For purposes of the application described in paragraph (1):

(A) Eligible employee

The term "eligible employee" means an eligible employee of an agency or school described in paragraph (1).

(B) Employer

The term "employer" means an agency or school described in paragraph (1).

(b) Leave does not violate certain other federal laws

A local educational agency and a private elementary or secondary school shall not be in violation of the Individuals with Disabilities Education Act [20 U.S.C. § 1400 et seq.], section 504 of the Rehabilitation Act of 1973 [29 U.S.C. § 794], or title VI of the Civil Rights Act of 1964 [42 U.S.C. § 2000d et seq.], solely as a result of an eligible employee of such agency or school exercising the rights of such employee under this title.

(c) Intermittent leave or leave on a reduced schedule for instructional employees

(1) In general

Subject to paragraph (2), in any case in which an eligible employee employed principally in an instructional capacity by any such educational agency or school requests leave under subparagraph (C) or (D) of section 2612 (a)(1) of this title that is foreseeable based on planned medical treatment and the employee would be on leave for greater than 20 percent of the total number of working days in the period during which the leave would extend, the agency or school may require that such employee elect either—

(A) to take leave for periods of a particular duration, not to exceed the duration of the planned medical treatment; or

(B) to transfer temporarily to an available alternative position offered by the employer for which the employee is qualified, and that—

(i) has equivalent pay and benefits; and

(ii) better accommodates recurring periods of leave than the regular employment position of the employee.

(2) Application

The elections described in subparagraphs (A) and (B) of paragraph (1) shall apply only with respect to an eligible employee who complies with section 2612(e)(2) of this title.

(d) Rules applicable to periods near the conclusion of an academic term

The following rules shall apply with respect to periods of leave near the conclusion of an academic term in the case of any eligible employee employed principally in an instructional capacity by any such educational agency or school:

(1) Leave more than 5 weeks prior to end of term

If the eligible employee begins leave under section 2612 of this title more than 5 weeks prior to the end of the academic term, the agency or school may require the employee to continue taking leave until the end of such term, if—

(A) the leave is of at least 3 weeks duration; and

(B) the return to employment would occur during the 3–week period before the end of such term.

(2) Leave less than 5 weeks prior to end of term

If the eligible employee begins leave under subparagraph (A), (B), or (C) of section 2612(a)(1) of this title during the period that commences 5 weeks prior to the end of the academic term, the agency or school may require the employee to continue taking leave until the end of such term, if—

(A) the leave is of greater than 2 weeks duration; and

(B) the return to employment would occur during the 2–week period before the end of such term.

(3) Leave less than 3 weeks prior to end of term

If the eligible employee begins leave under subparagraph (A), (B), or (C) of section 2612(1) of this title during the period that commences 3 weeks prior to the end of the academic term and the duration of the leave is greater than 5 working days, the agency or school may require the employee to continue to take leave until the end of such term.

(e) Restoration to equivalent employment position

For purposes of determinations under section 2614(a)(1)(B) of this title (relating to the restoration of an eligible employee to an equivalent position), in the case of a local educational agency or a private elementary or secondary school, such determination shall be made on the basis of established school board policies and practices, private school policies and practices, and collective bargaining agreements.

(f) Reduction of the amount of liability

If a local educational agency or a private elementary or secondary school that has violated this title proves to the satisfaction of the court that the agency, school, or department had reasonable grounds for believing that the underlying act or omission was not a violation of this title, such court may, in the discretion of the court, reduce the amount of the liability provided for under section 2617(a)(1)(A) of this title to the amount and interest determined under clauses (i) and (ii), respectively, of such section.

Sec. 109 [29 U.S.C. § 2619]. Notice

(a) In general

Each employer shall post and keep posted, in conspicuous places on the premises of the employer where notices to employees and applicants for employment are customarily posted, a notice, to be prepared or approved by the Secretary, setting forth excerpts from, or summaries of, the pertinent provisions of this title and information pertaining to the filing of a charge.

(b) Penalty

Any employer that willfully violates this section may be assessed a civil money penalty not to exceed $100 for each separate offense.

* * *

TITLE III—MISCELLANEOUS PROVISIONS

Sec. 401 [29 U.S.C. § 2651]. Effect on other laws

(a) Federal and state antidiscrimination laws

Nothing in this Act or any amendment made by this Act shall be construed to modify or affect any Federal or State law prohibiting discrimination on the basis of race, religion, color, national origin, sex, age, or disability.

(b) State and local laws

Nothing in this Act or any amendment made by this Act shall be construed to supersede any provision of any State or local law that provides greater family or medical leave rights than the rights established under this Act or any amendment made by this Act.

Sec. 402 [29 U.S.C. § 2652]. Effect on existing employment benefits

(a) More protective

Nothing in this Act or any amendment made by this Act shall be construed to diminish the obligation of an employer to comply with any collective bargaining agreement or any employment benefit program or plan that provides greater family or medical leave rights to employees than the rights established under this Act or any amendment made by this Act.

(b) Less protective

The rights established for employees under this Act or any amendment made by this Act shall not be diminished by any collective bargaining agreement or any employment benefit program or plan.

Sec. 403 [29 U.S.C. § 2653]. Encouragement of more generous leave policies

Nothing in this Act or any amendment made by this Act shall be construed to discourage employers from adopting or retaining leave policies more generous than any policies that comply with the requirements under this Act or any amendment made by this Act.

Sec. 404 [29 U.S.C. § 2654]. Regulations

The Secretary of Labor shall prescribe such regulations as are necessary to carry out title I and this title not later than 120 days after the date of the enactment of this Act.

* * *

IMMIGRATION REFORM AND CONTROL ACT OF 1986
8 U.S.C. § 1324b

Sec. 1324b. Unfair Immigration–Related Employment Practices

(a) Prohibition of discrimination based on national origin or citizenship status

(1) General rule

It is an unfair immigration-related employment practice for a person or other entity to discriminate against any individual (other than an unauthorized alien, as defined in section 1324a(h)(3) of this title) with respect to the hiring, or recruitment or referral for a fee, of the individual for employment or the discharging of the individual from employment—

(A) because of such individual's national origin, or

(B) in the case of a protected individual (as defined in paragraph (3)), because of such individual's citizenship status.

(2) Exceptions

Paragraph (1) shall not apply to—

(A) a person or other entity that employs three or fewer employees,

(B) a person's or entity's discrimination because of an individual's national origin if the discrimination with respect to that person or entity and that individual is covered under section 703 of the Civil Rights Act of 1964 [42 U.S.C. § 2000e–2], or

(C) discrimination because of citizenship status which is otherwise required in order to comply with law, regulation, or executive order, or required by Federal, State, or local government contract, or which the Attorney General determines to be essential for an employer to do business with an agency or department of the Federal, State, or local government.

(3) "Protected individual" defined

As used in paragraph (1), the term "protected individual" means an individual who—

(A) is a citizen or national of the United States, or

(B) is an alien who is lawfully admitted for permanent residence, is granted the status of an alien lawfully admitted for temporary residence under section 210(1), 210A(a), or 245A(a)(1), is admitted as a refugee under section 207; or is granted asylum under section 208, but does not include (i) an alien who fails to apply for naturalization within six months of the date the alien first becomes eligible (by virtue of period of lawful permanent residence) to apply for naturalization or, if later, within six months after November 6, 1986, and (ii) an alien who has applied on a timely basis, but has not been naturalized as a citizen within 2 years after the date of the application, unless the alien can establish that the alien is actively pursuing naturalization, except that time consumed in the Service's processing the application shall not be counted toward the 2–year period.

(4) Additional exception providing right to prefer equally qualified citizens

Notwithstanding any other provision of this section, it is not an unfair immigration-related employment practice for a person or other entity to prefer to hire, recruit, or refer an individual who is a citizen or national of the United States over another individual who is an alien if the two individuals are equally qualified.

(5) Prohibition of intimidation or retaliation

It is also an unfair immigration-related employment practice for a person or other entity to intimidate, threaten, coerce, or retaliate against any individual for the purpose of interfering with any right or privilege secured under this section or because the individual intends to file or has filed a charge or a complaint, testified, assisted, or participated in any manner in an investigation, proceeding, or hearing under this section. An individual so intimidated, threatened, coerced, or retaliated against shall be considered, for purposes of subsections (d) and (g) of this section, to have been discriminated against.

(6) Treatment of certain documentary practices as employment practices

For purposes of paragraph (1), a person's or other entity's request, for purposes of satisfying the requirements of section 1324a(b) of this title, for more or different documents than are required under such section or refusing to honor documents tendered that on their face reasonably appear to be genuine shall be treated as an unfair immigration-related employment practice relating to the hiring of individuals.

(b) Charges of violations

(1) In general

Except as provided in paragraph (2), any person alleging that the person is adversely affected directly by an unfair immigration-related employment practice (or a person on that person's behalf) or an officer of the Service alleging that an unfair immigration-related employment practice has occurred or is occurring may file a charge respecting such practice or violation with the Special Counsel (appointed under subsection (c)). Charges shall be in writing under oath or affirmation and shall contain such information as the Attorney General requires. The Special Counsel by certified mail shall serve a notice of the charge (including the date, place, and circumstances of the alleged unfair immigration-related employment practice) on the person or entity involved within 10 days.

(2) No overlap with EEOC complaints

No charge may be filed respecting an unfair immigration-related employment practice described in subsection (a)(1)(A) if a charge with respect to that practice based on the same set of facts has been filed with the Equal Employment Opportunity Commission under title VII of the Civil Rights Act of 1964 [42 U.S.C. § 2000e et seq.], unless the charge is dismissed as being outside the scope of such title. No charge respecting an employment practice may be filed with the Equal Employment Opportunity Commission under such title if a charge with respect to such practice based on the same set of facts has been filed under this subsection, unless the change is dismissed under this section as being outside the scope of this section.

(c) Special counsel

(1) Appointment

The President shall appoint, by and with the advice the consent of the Senate, a Special Counsel for Immigration–Related Unfair Employment Practices (hereinafter in this section referred to as the "Special Counsel") within the Department of Justice to serve for a term of four years. In the case of a vacancy in the office of the Special Counsel the President may designate the officer or employee who shall act as Special Counsel during such vacancy.

(2) Duties

The Special Counsel shall be responsible for investigation of charges and issuance of complaints under this section and in respect of the prosecution of all such complaints before administrative law judges and the exercise of certain functions under subsection (j)(1) of this section.

(3) Compensation

The Special Counsel is entitled to receive compensation at a rate not to exceed the rate now or hereafter provided for grade GS–17 of the General Schedule, under section 5332 of title 5, United States Code.

(4) Regional offices

The Special Counsel, in accordance with regulations of the Attorney General, shall establish such regional offices as may be necessary to carry out his duties.

(d) Investigation of charges

(1) By special counsel

The Special Counsel shall investigate each charge received and, within 120 days of the date of the receipt of the charge, determine whether or not there is reasonable cause to believe that the charge is true and whether or not to bring a complaint with respect to the charge before an administrative law judge. The Special Counsel may, on his own initiative, conduct investigations respecting unfair immigration-related employment practices and, based on such an investigation and subject to paragraph (3), file a complaint before such judge.

(2) Private actions

If the Special Counsel, after receiving such a charge respecting an unfair immigration-related employment practice which alleges knowing and intentional discriminatory activity or a pattern or practice of discriminatory activity, has not filed a complaint before an administrative law judge with respect to such charge within such 120–day period, the Special Counsel shall notify the person making the charge of the determination not to file such a complaint during such period and the person making the charge may (subject to paragraph (3)) file a complaint directly before such a judge within 90 days after the date of receipt of the notice. The Special Counsel's failure to file such a complaint within such 120–day period shall not affect the right of the Special Counsel to investigate the charge or to bring a complaint before an administrative law judge during such 90–day period.

(3) Time limitations of complaints

No complaint may be filed respecting any unfair immigration-related employment practice occurring more than 180 days prior to the date of the filing of the charge with the Special Counsel. This subparagraph shall not prevent the subsequent amending of a charge or complaint under subsection (e)(1) of this section.

(e) Hearings

(1) Notice

Whenever a complaint is made that a person or entity has engaged in or is engaging in any such unfair immigration-related employment practice, an administrative law judge shall have power to issue and cause to be served upon such person or entity a copy of the complaint and a notice of hearing before the judge at a place therein fixed, not less than five days after the serving of the complaint. Any such complaint may be amended by the judge conducting the hearing, upon the motion of the party filing the complaint, in the judge's discretion at any time prior to the issuance of an order based thereon. The person or entity so complained of shall have the right to file an answer to the original or amended complaint and to appear in person or otherwise and give testimony at the place and time fixed in the complaint.

(2) Judges hearing cases

Hearings on complaints under this subsection shall be considered before administrative law judges who are specially designated by the Attorney General as having special training respecting employment discrimination and, to the extent practicable, before such judges who only consider cases under this section.

(3) Complainant as party

Any person filing a charge with the Special Counsel respecting an unfair immigration-related employment practice shall be considered a party to any complaint before an administrative law judge respecting such practice and any subsequent appeal respecting that complaint. In the discretion of the judge conducting the hearing, any other person may be allowed to intervene in the proceeding and to present testimony.

(f) Testimony and authority of hearing officers

(1) Testimony

The testimony taken by the administrative law judge shall be reduced to writing. Thereafter, the judge, in his discretion, upon notice may provide for the taking of further testimony or hear argument.

(2) Authority of administrative law judges

In conducting investigations and hearings under this subsection and in accordance with regulations of the Attorney General, the Special Counsel and administrative law judges shall have reasonable access to examine evidence of any person or entity being investigated. The administrative law judges by subpoena may compel the attendance of witnesses and the production of evidence at any designated place or hearing. In case of contumacy or refusal to obey a subpoena lawfully issued under this paragraph and upon application of the administrative law judge, an appropriate district court of the United States may issue an order requiring compliance with such subpoena and any failure to obey such order may be punished by such court as a contempt thereof.

(g) Determinations

(1) Order

The administrative law judge shall issue and cause to be served on the parties to the proceeding an order, which shall be final unless appealed as provided under subsection (i) of this section.

(2) Orders finding violations

(A) In general

If, upon the preponderance of the evidence, an administrative law judge determines that any person or entity named in the complaint has engaged in or is engaging in any such unfair immigration-related employment practice, then the judge shall state his findings of fact and shall issue and cause to be served on such person or entity an order which requires such person or entity to cease and desist from such unfair immigration-related employment practice.

(B) Contents of order

Such an order also may require the person or entity—

(i) to comply with the requirements of section 1324a(b) of this title with respect to individuals hired (or recruited or referred for employment for a fee) during a period of up to three years;

(ii) to retain for the period referred to in clause (i) and only for purposes consistent with section 1324a(b) of this title, the name and address of each individual who applies, in person or in writing, for hiring for an existing position, or for recruiting or referring for a fee, for employment in the United States;

(iii) to hire individuals directly and adversely affected, with or without back pay;

(iv)(I) except as provided in subclause (II) through (iv), to pay a civil penalty of not less than $250 and not more than $2,000 for each individual discriminated against, and

(II) except as provided in subclauses (III) and (IV), in the case of a person or entity previously subject to a single order under this paragraph, to pay a civil penalty of not less than $2,000 and not more than $5,000 for each individual discriminated against,

(III) except as provided in subclause (IV), in the case of a person or entity previously subject to more than one order under this paragraph, to pay a civil penalty of not less than $3,000 and not more than $10,000 for each individual discriminated against, and

(IV) in the case of an unfair immigration-related employment practice described in subsection (a)(6) of this section, to pay a civil penalty of not less than $100 and not more than $1,000 for each individual discriminated against;

(v) to post notices to employees about their rights under this section and employers' obligations under section 1324a of this title;

(vi) to educate all personnel involved in hiring and complying with this section or section 1324a of this title about the requirements of this section or such section;

(vii) to remove (in an appropriate case) a false performance review or false warning from an employee's personnel file; and

(viii) to lift (in an appropriate case) any restrictions on an employee's assignments, work shifts, or movements.

(C) Limitation on back pay remedy

In providing a remedy under subparagraph (B)(iii), back pay liability shall not accrue from a date more than two years prior to the date of the filing of a charge with Special Counsel. Interim earnings or amounts earnable with reasonable diligence by the individual or individuals discriminated against shall operate to reduce the back pay otherwise allowable under such paragraph. No order shall require the hiring of an individual as an employee or the payment to an individual of any back pay, if the individual was refused employment for any reason other than discrimination on account of national origin or citizenship status.

(D) Treatment of distinct entities

In applying this subsection in the case of a person or entity composed of distinct, physically separate subdivisions each of which provides separately for the hiring, recruiting, or referring for employment, without reference to the practices of, and not under the control of or common control with, another subdivision, each such subdivision shall be considered a separate person or entity.

(3) Orders not finding violations

If upon the preponderance of evidence an administrative law judge determines that the person or entity named in the complaint has not engaged and is not engaging in any such unfair immigration-related employment practice, then the judge shall state his findings of fact and shall issue an order dismissing the complaint.

(h) Awarding of attorney's fees

In any complaint respecting an unfair immigration-related employment practice, an administrative law judge, in the judge's discretion, may allow a prevailing party, other than the United States, a reasonable attorney's fee, if the losing party's argument is without reasonable foundation in law and fact.

(i) Review of final orders

(1) In general

Not later than 60 days after the entry of such final order, any person aggrieved by such final order may seek a review of such order in the United States court of appeals for the circuit in which the violation is alleged to have occurred or in which the employer resides or transacts business.

(2) Further review

Upon the filing of the record with the court, the jurisdiction of the court shall be exclusive and its judgment shall be final, except that the same shall be subject to review by the Supreme Court of the United States upon writ of certiorari or certification as provided in section 1254 of title 28.

(j) Court enforcement of administrative orders

(1) In general

If an order of the agency is not appealed under subsection (i)(1), the Special Counsel (or, if the Special Counsel fails to act, the person filing the charge) may petition the United States district court for the district in which a violation of the order is alleged to have occurred, or in which the respondent resides or transacts business, for the enforcement of the order of the administrative law judge, by filing in such court a written petition praying that such order be enforced.

(2) Court enforcement order

Upon the filing of such petition, the court shall have jurisdiction to make and enter a decree enforcing the order of the administrative law judge. In such a proceeding, the order of the administrative law judge shall not be subject to review.

(3) Enforcement decree in original review

If, upon appeal of an order under subsection (i)(1) of this section, the United States court of appeals does not reverse such order, such court shall have the jurisdiction to make and enter a decree enforcing the order of the administrative law judge.

(4) Awarding of attorney's fees

In any judicial proceeding under subsection (i) of this section or this subsection, the court, in its discretion, may allow a prevailing party, other than the United States, a reasonable attorney's fee as part of costs but only if the losing party's argument is without reasonable foundation in law and fact.

(k) Termination dates

(1) This section shall not apply to discrimination in hiring, recruiting, referring, or discharging of individuals occurring after the date of any termination of the provisions of section 1324a of this title, under subsection (*l*) of that section.

(2) the provisions of this section shall terminate 30 calendar days after receipt of the last report required to be transmitted under section 1324a of this title (j) if—

(A) the Comptroller General determines, and so reports in such report that—

(i) no significant discrimination has resulted, against citizens or nationals of the United States or against any eligible workers seeking employment, from the implementation of section 1324a of this title, or

(ii) such section has created an unreasonable burden on employers hiring such workers; and

(B) there has been enacted, within such period of 30 calendar days, a joint resolution stating in substance that the Congress approves the findings of the Comptroller General contained in such report.

The provisions of subsections (m) and (n) of section 1324a of this title shall apply to any joint resolution under subparagraph (B) in the same manner as they apply to a joint resolution under subsection (*l*) of such section.

(*l*) Dissemination of information concerning anti-discrimination provisions

(1) Not later than 3 months after November 29, 1990, the Special Counsel, in cooperation with the chairman of the Equal Employment Opportunity Commission, the Secretary of Labor, and the Administrator of the Small Business Administration, shall conduct a campaign to disseminate information respecting the rights and remedies prescribed under this section and under title VII of the Civil Rights Act of 1964 [42 U.S.C. § 2000e et seq.] in connection with unfair immigration-related employment practices. Such campaign shall be aimed at increasing the knowledge of employers, employees, and the general public concerning employer and employee rights, responsibilities, and remedies under this section and such title.

* * *

GLASS CEILING ACT OF 1991[1]
Pub. L. No. 102–166, 105 Stat. 1081 (1991)
(Codified at 42 U.S.C. § 2000e)

Sec. 201. Short title

This title may be cited as the "Glass Ceiling Act of 1991."

Sec. 202. Findings and purpose

(a) Findings.—Congress finds that—

(1) despite a dramatically growing presence in the workplace, women and minorities remain underrepresented in management and decisionmaking positions in business;

(2) artificial barriers exist to the advancement of women and minorities in the workplace;

(3) United States corporations are increasingly relying on women and minorities to meet employment requirements and are increasingly aware of the advantages derived from a diverse work force;

(4) the "Glass Ceiling Initiative" undertaken by the Department of Labor, including the release of the report entitled "Report on the Glass Initiative," has been instrumental in raising public awareness of—

(A) the underrepresentation of women and minorities at the management and decisionmaking levels in the United States work force;

(B) the underrepresentation of women and minorities in line functions in the United States work force;

(C) the lack of access for qualified women and minorities to credential-building developmental opportunities; and

(D) the desirability of eliminating artificial barriers to the advancement of women and minorities to such levels;

(5) the establishment of a commission to examine issues raised by the Glass Ceiling Initiative would help—

(A) focus greater attention on the importance of eliminating artificial barriers to the advancement of women and minorities to management and decisionmaking positions in business; and

(B) promote work force diversity;

(6) a comprehensive study that includes analysis of the manner in which management and decisionmaking positions are filled, the developmental and skill-enhancing practices used to foster the necessary qualifi-

1. Enacted as Title II of the Civil Rights Act of 1991.

cations for advancement, and the compensation programs and reward structures utilized in the corporate sector would assist in the establishment of practices and policies promoting opportunities for, and eliminating artificial barriers to, the advancement of women and minorities to management and decisionmaking positions; and

(7) a national award recognizing employers whose practices and policies promote opportunities for, and eliminate artificial barriers to, the advancement of women and minorities will foster the advancement of women and minorities into higher level positions by—

(A) helping to encourage United States companies to modify practices and policies to promote opportunities for, and eliminate artificial barriers to, the upward mobility of women and minorities; and

(B) providing specific guidance for other United States employers that wish to learn how to revise practices and policies to improve the access and employment opportunities of women and minorities; and

(b) Purpose.—The purpose of this title is to establish

(1) a Glass Ceiling Commission to study—

(A) the manner in which business fills management and decisionmaking positions;

(B) the developmental and skill-enhancing practices used to foster the necessary qualifications for advancement into such positions; and

(C) the compensation programs and reward structures currently utilized in the workplace; and

(2) an annual award for excellence in promoting a more diverse skilled work force at the management and decisionmaking levels in business.

Sec. 203. Establishment of Glass Ceiling Commission

(a) In general.—There is established a Glass Ceiling Commission (referred to in this title as the "Commission"), to conduct a study and prepare recommendations concerning—

(1) eliminating artificial barriers to the advancement of women and minorities; and

(2) increasing the opportunities and developmental experiences of women and minorities to foster advancement of women and minorities to management and decisionmaking positions in business.

(b) Membership.—

(1) Composition.—The Commission shall be composed of 21 members, including—

(A) six individuals appointed by the President;

(B) six individuals appointed jointly by the Speaker of the House of Representatives and the Majority Leader of the Senate;

(C) one individual appointed by the Majority Leader of the House of Representatives;

(D) one individual appointed by the Minority Leader of the House of Representatives;

(E) one individual appointed by the Majority Leader of the Senate;

(F) one individual appointed by the Minority Leader of the Senate;

(G) two Members of the House of Representatives appointed jointly by the Majority Leader and the Minority Leader of the House of Representatives;

(H) two Members of the Senate appointed jointly by the Majority Leader and the Minority Leader of the Senate; and

(I) the Secretary of Labor.

(2) Considerations.—In making appointments under subparagraphs (A) and (B) of paragraph (1), the appointing authority shall consider the background of the individuals, including whether the individuals—

(A) are members of organizations representing women and minorities, and other related interest groups;

(B) hold management or decisionmaking positions in corporations or other business entities recognized as leaders on issues relating to equal employment opportunity; and

(C) possess academic expertise or other recognized ability regarding employment issues.

(3) Balance.—In making the appointments under subparagraphs (A) and (B) of paragraph (1), each appointment authority shall seek to include an appropriate balance of appointees from among the groups of appointees described in subparagraphs (A), (B) and (C) of paragraph (2).

(c) Chairperson.—The Secretary of Labor shall serve as the Chairperson of the Commission.

(d) Term of office.—Members shall be appointed for the life of the Commission.

(e) Vacancies.—Any vacancy occurring in the membership of the Commission shall be filled in the same manner as the original appointment for the position being vacated. The vacancy shall not affect the power of the remaining members to execute the duties of the Commission.

(f) Meetings.—

(1) Meetings prior to completion of report.—The Commission shall meet not fewer than five times in connection with and pending the completion of the report described in section 204(b). The Commission shall hold additional meetings if the Chairperson or a majority of the members of the Commission request the additional meetings in writing.

(2) Meetings after completion of report.—The Commission shall meet once each year after the completion of the report described in section 204(b). The Commission shall hold additional meetings if the Chairperson or a majority of the members of the Commission request the additional meetings in writing.

(g) Quorum.—A majority of the Commission shall constitute a quorum for the transaction of business.

(h) Compensation and expenses.—

(1) Compensation.—Each member of the Commission who is not an employee of the Federal Government shall receive compensation at the daily equivalent of the rate specified for level V of the Executive Schedule under section 5316 of title 5, United States Code, for each day the member is engaged in the performance of duties for the Commission, including attendance at meetings and conferences of the Commission, and travel to conduct the duties of the Commission.

(2) Travel expenses.—Each member of the Commission shall receive travel expenses, including per diem in lieu of subsistence, at rates authorized for employees of agencies under subchapter I of chapter 57 of title 5, United States Code, for each day the member is engaged in the performance of duties away from the home or regular place of business of the member.

(3) Employment status.—A member of the Commission, who is not otherwise an employee of the Federal Government, shall not be deemed to be an employee of the Federal Government except for the purposes of—

(A) the tort claims provisions of chapter 171 of title 28, United States Code; and

(B) subchapter I of chapter 81 of title 5, United States Code, relating to compensation for work injuries.

Sec. 204. Research on advancement of women and minorities to management and decisionmaking positions in business

(a) Advancement study.—The Commission shall conduct a study of opportunities for, and artificial barriers to, the advancement of women and minorities to management and decisionmaking positions in business. In conducting the study, the Commission shall—

(1) examine the preparedness of women and minorities to advance to management and decisionmaking positions in business;

(2) examine the opportunities for women and minorities to advance to management and decisionmaking positions in business;

(3) conduct basic research into the practices, policies, and manner in which management and decisionmaking positions in business are filled;

(4) conduct comparative research of businesses and industries in which women and minorities are promoted to management and decisionmaking positions, and businesses and industries in which women and minorities are not promoted to management and decisionmaking positions;

(5) compile a synthesis of available research on programs and practices that have successfully led to the advancement of women and minorities to management and decisionmaking positions in business, including training programs, rotational assignments, developmental programs, reward programs, employee benefit structures, and family leave policies; and

(6) examine any other issues and information relating to the advancement of women and minorities to management and decisionmaking positions in business.

(b) Report.—Not later than 15 months after the date of the enactment of this Act [Nov. 21, 1991], the Commission shall prepare and submit to the President and the appropriate committees of Congress a written report containing—

(1) the findings and conclusions of the Commission resulting from the study conducted under subsection (a); and

(2) recommendations based on the findings and conclusions described in paragraph (1) relating to the promotion of opportunities for, and elimination of artificial barriers to, the advancement of women and minorities to management and decisionmaking positions in business, including recommendations for—

(A) policies and practices to fill vacancies at the management and decisionmaking levels;

(B) developmental practices and procedures to ensure that women and minorities have access to opportunities to gain the exposure, skills, and expertise necessary to assume management and decisionmaking positions;

(C) compensation programs and reward structures utilized to reward and retain key employees; and

(D) the use of enforcement (including such enforcement techniques as litigation, complaint investigations, compliance reviews, conciliation, administrative regulations, policy guidance, technical assistance, training, and public education) of Federal equal employment opportunity laws by Federal agencies as a means of eliminating artificial barriers to the advancement of women and minorities in employment.

(c) Additional study.—The Commission may conduct such additional study of the advancement of women and minorities to management and decisionmaking positions in business as a majority of the members of the Commission determines to be necessary.

Sec. 205. Establishment of the National Award for Diversity and Excellence in American Executive Management

(a) In general.—There is established the National Award for Diversity and Excellence in American Executive Management, which shall be evidenced by a medal bearing the inscription "Frances Perkins—Elizabeth Hanford Dole National Award for Diversity and Excellence in American Executive Management." The medal shall be of such design and materials, and bear such additional inscriptions, as the Commission may prescribe.

(b) Criteria for qualification.—To qualify to receive an award under this section a business shall—

(1) submit a written application to the Commission, at such time, in such manner, and containing such information as the Commission may require, including at a minimum information that demonstrates that the business has made substantial effort to promote the opportunities and developmental experiences of women and minorities to foster advancement to management and decisionmaking positions within the business, including the elimination of artificial barriers to the advancement of women and minorities, and deserves special recognition as a consequence; and

(2) meet such additional requirements and specifications as the Commission determines to be appropriate.

(c) Making and presentation of award.—

(1) Award.—After receiving recommendations from the Commission, the President or the designated representative of the President shall annually present the award described in subsection (a) to businesses that meet the qualifications described in subsection (b).

(2) Presentation.—The President or the designated representative of the President shall present the award with such ceremonies as the President or the designated representative of the President may determine to be appropriate.

(3) Publicity.—A business that receives an award under this section may publicize the receipt of the award and use the award in its advertising, if the business agrees to help other United States businesses improve with respect to the promotion of opportunities and developmental experiences of women and minorities to foster the advancement of women and minorities to management and decisionmaking positions.

(d) Business.—For the purposes of this section, the term "business" includes—

(1)(A) a corporation including non-profit corporations;

(B) a partnership;

(C) a professional association;

(D) a labor organization; and

(E) a business entity similar to an entity described in subparagraphs (A) through (D);

(2) an education referral program, a training program, such as an apprenticeship or management training program or a similar program; and

(3) a joint program formed by a combination of any entities described in paragraph 1 or 2.

Sec. 206. Powers of the Commission

(a) In general.—The Commission is authorized to—

(1) hold such hearings and sit and act at such times;

(2) take such testimony;

(3) have such printing and binding done;

(4) enter into such contracts and other arrangements;

(5) make such expenditures; and

(6) take such other actions; as the Commission may determine to be necessary to carry out the duties of the Commission.

(b) Oaths.—Any member of the Commission may administer oaths or affirmations to witnesses appearing before the Commission.

(c) Obtaining information from Federal agencies.—The Commission may secure directly from any Federal agency such information as the Commission may require to carry out its duties.

(d) Voluntary service.—Notwithstanding section 1342 of title 31, United States Code, the Chairperson of the Commission may accept for the Commission voluntary services provided by a member of the Commission.

(e) Gifts and donations.—The Commission may accept, use, and dispose of gifts or donations of property in order to carry out the duties of the Commission.

(f) Use of mail.—The Commission may use the United States mails in the same manner and under the same conditions as Federal agencies.

Sec. 207. Confidentiality Of Information

(a) Individual business information.—

(1) In General.—Except as provided in paragraph (2), and notwithstanding section 552 of title 5, United States Code, in carrying out the duties of the Commission, including the duties described in sections 204 and 205, the Commission shall maintain the confidentiality of all information that concerns—

(A) the employment practices and procedures of individual businesses; or

(B) individual employees of the business.

(2) Consent.—The content of any information described in paragraph (1) may be disclosed with the prior written consent of the business or employee, as the case may be, with respect to which the information is maintained.

(b) Aggregate information.—In carrying out the duties of the Commission, the Commission may disclose—

(1) information about the aggregate employment practices or procedures of a class or group of businesses; and

(2) information about the aggregate characteristics of employees of the business, and related aggregate information about the employees.

Sec. 208. Staff and Consultants

(a) Staff.—

(1) Appointment and compensation.—The Commission may appoint and determine the compensation of such staff as the Commission determines to be necessary to carry out the duties of the Commission.

(2) Limitations.—The rate of compensation for each staff member shall not exceed the daily equivalent of the rate specified for level V of the Executive Schedule under section 5316 of title 5, United States Code, for each day the staff member is engaged in the performance of duties for the Commission. The Commission may otherwise appoint and determine the compensation of staff without regard to the provisions of title 5, United States Code, that govern appointments in the competitive service, and the provisions of chapter 51 and subchapter III of chapter 53 of title 5, United States Code, that relate to classification and General Schedule pay rates.

(b) Experts and consultants.—The Chairperson of the Commission may obtain such temporary and intermittent services of experts and consultants and compensate the experts and consultants in accordance with section 31019(b) of title 5, United States Code, as the Commission determines to be necessary to carry out the duties of the Commission.

(c) Detail of Federal employees.—On the request of the Chairperson of the Commission, the head of any Federal agency shall detail, without reimbursement, any of the personnel of the agency to the Commission to assist the Commission in carrying out its duties. Any detail shall not interrupt or otherwise affect the civil service status or privileges of the Federal employee.

(d) Technical assistance.—On the request of the Chairperson of the Commission, the head of a Federal agency shall provide such technical assistance to the Commission as the Commission determines to be necessary to carry out its duties.

Sec. 209. Authorization of Appropriations

There are authorized to be appropriated to the Commission such sums as may be necessary to carry out the provisions of this title. The sums shall remain available until expended, without fiscal year limitation.

Sec. 210. Termination

(a) Commission.—Notwithstanding section 15 of the Federal Advisory Committee Act (5 U.S.C. App.), the Commission shall terminate 4 years after the date of the enactment of this Act [Nov. 21, 1991].

(b) Award.—The authority to make awards under section 205 shall terminate 4 years after the date of the enactment of this Act.

CONGRESSIONAL ACCOUNTABILITY ACT OF 1995
2 U.S.C. §§ 1301–1317, 1361, 1381, 1401–1408, 1415–1416, 1432

Sec. 101 [2 U.S.C. § 1301]. Definitions

Except as otherwise specifically provided in this Chapter, as used in this Act:

(1) Board

The term "Board" means the Board of Directors of the Office of Compliance.

(2) Chair

The term "Chair" means the Chair of the Board of Directors of the Office of Compliance.

(3) Covered employee

The term "covered employee" means any employee of—

(A) the House of Representatives;

(B) the Senate;

(C) the Capitol Guide Service;

(D) the Capitol Police;

(E) the Congressional Budget Office;

(F) the Office of the Architect of the Capitol;

(G) the Office of the Attending Physician;

(H) the Office of Compliance; or

(I) the Office of Technology Assessment.

(4) Employee

The term "employee" includes an applicant for employment and a former employee.

(5) Employee of the Office of the Architect of the Capitol

The term "employee of the Office of the Architect of the Capitol" includes any employee of the Office of the Architect of the Capitol, the Botanic Garden, or the Senate Restaurants.

(6) Employee of the Capitol Police

The term "employee of the Capitol Police" includes any member or officer of the Capitol Police.

(7) Employee of the House of Representatives

The term "employee of the House of Representatives" includes an individual occupying a position the pay for which is disbursed by the Clerk of the House of Representatives, or another official designated by the House of Representatives, or any employment position in an entity that is paid with funds derived from the clerk-hire allowance of the House of Representative but not any such individual employed by any entity listed in subparagraphs (C) through (I) of paragraph (3).

(8) Employee of the Senate

The term "employee of the Senate" includes any employee whose pay is disbursed by the Secretary of the Senate, but not any such individual employed by any entity listed in subparagraph (C) through (I) of paragraph (3).

(9) Employing office

The term "employing office" means—

(A) the personal office of a Member of the House of Representatives or of a Senator;

(B) a committee of the House of Representatives or the Senate or a joint committee;

(C) any other office headed by a person with the final authority to appoint, hire, discharge, and set the terms, conditions, or privileges of the employment of an employee of the House of Representatives or Senate; or

(D) the Capitol Guide Board, the Capitol Police Board, the Congressional Budget Office, the Office of the Architect of the Capitol, the Office of the Attending Physician, the Office of Compliance, and the Office of Technology Assessment.

(10) Executive Director

The term "Executive Director" means the Executive Director of the Office of Compliance.

(11) General Counsel

The term "General Counsel" means the General Counsel of the Office of Compliance.

(12) Office

The term "Office" means the Office of Compliance.

Sec. 102 [42 U.S.C. § 1302]. Application of laws

(a) Laws made applicable

The following laws shall apply, as prescribed by this Act, to the legislative branch of the Federal Government:

(1) The Fair Labor Standards Act of 1938 (29 U.S.C. § 201 et seq.).

(2) Title VII of the Civil Rights Act of 1964 (42 U.S.C. § 2000e et seq.).

(3) The American with Disabilities Act of 1990 (42 U.S.C. § 12101 et seq.).

(4) The Age Discrimination in Employment Act of 1967 (29 U.S.C. § 621 et seq.).

(5) The Family and Medical Leave Act of 1993 (29 U.S.C. § 2611 et seq.).

(6) The Occupational Safety and Health Act of 1970 (29 U.S.C. § 651 et seq.).

(7) Chapter 71 (relating to Federal service labor-management relations) of title 5.

(8) The Employee Polygraph Protection Act of 1988 (29 U.S.C. § 2001 et seq.).

(9) The Worker Adjustment and Retraining Notification Act (29 U.S.C. § 2101 et seq.).

(10) The Rehabilitation Act of 1973 (29 U.S.C. § 701 et seq.).

(11) Chapter 43 (relating to veterans' employment and reemployment) of title 38

(b) Laws which may be made applicable

(1) In general

The Board shall review provisions of Federal Law (including regulations) relating to

(A) the terms and conditions of employment (including hiring, promotion, demotion, termination, salary, wages, overtime compensation, benefits, work assignments or reassignments, grievance and disciplinary procedures, protection from discrimination in personnel actions, occupational health and safety, and family and medical and other leave) of employees, and

(B) access to public services and accommodations.

(2) Board report

Beginning on December 31, 1996 and every 2 years thereafter, the Board shall report on

(A) whether or to what degree the provisions described in paragraph (1) are applicable or inapplicable to the legislative branch, and

(B) with respect to provisions inapplicable to the legislative branch, whether such provisions should be made applicable to the legislative branch. The presiding officers of the House of Representatives and the Senate shall cause each such report to be printed in the Congressional Record and each such report shall be referred to the committees of the House of Representatives and Senate with jurisdiction.

(3) Reports of Congressional committees

Each report accompanying any bill or joint resolution relating to terms and conditions of employment or access to public services or accommodations reported by a committee of the House of Representatives or the Senate shall—

(A) describe the manner in which the provisions of the bill or joint resolution apply to the legislative branch; or

(B) in the case of a provision not applicable to the legislative branch, include a statement of the reasons the provision does not apply.

On the objection of any Member, it shall not be in order for the Senate or the House of Representatives to consider any such bill or joint resolution if the report of the committee on such a bill or joint resolution does not comply with the provisions of this paragraph. This paragraph may be waived in either House by majority vote of that House.

Sec. 201 [2 U.S.C. § 1311]. Rights and protections under Title VII of the Civil Rights Act of 1964, the Age Discrimination in Employment Act of 1967, the Rehabilitation Act of 1973, and Title I of the Americans with Disabilities Act of 1990

(a) Discriminatory practices prohibited

All personnel actions affecting covered employees shall be made free from any discrimination based on—

(1) race, color, religion, sex, or national origin, within the meaning of section 703 of the Civil Rights Act of 1964 (42 U.S.C. § 2000e–2).

(2) age, within the meaning of section 15 of the Age Discrimination in Employment Act of 1967 (29 U.S.C. § 633a); or

(3) disability, within the meaning of section 501 of the Rehabilitation Act of 1973 (29 U.S.C. § 791) and section 102 through 104 of the Americans with Disabilities Act of 1990 (42 U.S.C. §§ 12112–12114).

(b) Remedy

(1) Civil rights

The remedy for a violation of subsection (a)(1) shall be—

(A) such remedy as would be appropriate if awarded under section 706(g) of the Civil Rights Act of 1964 (42 § 2000–5(g)); and

(B) such compensatory damages as would be appropriate if awarded under section 1977 of the Revised Statutes (42 U.S.C. § 1981), or as would be appropriate if awarded under sections

1977A(a)(1), 1977A(b)(2), and, irrespective of the size of the employing office, 1977A(b)(3)(D) of the Revised Statutes (42 U.S.C. § 1981a(a)(1), 1981a(b)(2), and 1981a(b)(3)(D)).

(2) Age discrimination

The remedy for violation of subsection (a)(2) shall be—

(A) such remedy as would be appropriate if awarded under section 15(c) of the Age Discrimination in Employment Act of 1967 (29 U.S.C. § 633a(c)); and

(B) such liquidated damages as would be appropriate if awarded under section 7(b) of such Act (29 U.S.C. § 626(b)).

In addition, the waiver provisions of section 7(f) of such Act (29 U.S.C. § 626(f)) shall apply to covered employees.

(3) Disabilities discrimination

The remedy for violation of subsection (a)(3) shall be—

(A) such remedy as would be appropriate if awarded under section 505(a)(1) of the Rehabilitation Act of 1973 (29 U.S.C. § 794a(a)(1)) or section 107(a) of the Americans with Disabilities Act of 1990 (42 U.S.C. § 12117(a)); and

(B) such compensatory damages as would be appropriate if awarded under sections 1977A(a)(2), 1977A(a)(3), 1977A(b)(2), and, irrespective of the size of the employing office, 1977A(b)(3)(D) of the Revised Statutes (42 U.S.C. §§ 1981a(a)(2), 1981a(a)(3), 1981a(b)(2), and 1981a(b)(3)(D)).

(d) Effective date

This section shall take effect 1 year after the date of the enactment of this Act.

Sec. 202 [2 U.S.C. § 1312]. Rights and protections under the Family and Medical Leave Act of 1993

(a) Family and medical leave rights and protections provided

(1) In general

The rights and protections established by sections 101 through 105 of the Family and Medical Leave Act of 1993 (29 U.S.C. §§ 2611 through 2615) shall apply to covered employees.

(2) Definition.—For purposes of applications described in paragraph (1)—

(A) the term "employer" as used in the Family and Medical Leave Act of 1993 means any employing office, and

(B) the term "eligible employee" as used in the Family and Medical Leave Act of 1993 means a covered employee who has been employed in any employing office for 12 months and for at least 1,250 hours of employment during the previous 12 months.

(b) Remedy

The remedy for a violation of subsection (a) shall be such remedy, including liquidated damages, as would be appropriate if awarded under paragraph (1) of section 107(a) of the Family and Medical Leave Act of 1993 (29 U.S.C. § 2617(a)(1)).

* * *

Sec. 203 [2 U.S.C.§ 1313]. Rights and protections under the Fair Labor Standards Act of 1938

(a) Fair labor standards

(1) In general

The rights and protections established by subsection (a)(1) and (d) of section 6, section 7, and section 12(c) of the Fair Labor Standards Act of 1938 (29 U.S.C. § 206(a)(1) and (d), § 207, § 212(c)) shall apply to covered employees.

(2) Interns

For the purpose of this section, the term "covered employee" does not include an intern as defined in regulations under subsection (c).

(3) Compensatory time

Except as provided in regulation under subsection (c)(3), covered employees may not receive compensatory time in lieu of overtime compensation.

(b) Remedy

The remedy for a violation of subsection (a) shall be such remedy, including liquidated damages, as would be appropriate if awarded under section 16(b) of the Fair Labor Standards Act of 1938 (29 U.S.C. § 216(b)).

(c) Regulations to implement section

(1) In general

The Board shall, pursuant to section 304, issue regulations to implement this section.

(2) Agency regulations

Except as provided in paragraph (3), the regulations issued under paragraph (1) shall be the same as substantive regulations promulgated by the Secretary of Labor to implement the statutory provisions referred to in subsection (a) except insofar as the Board may determine, for good cause shown and stated together with the regulation, that a modification of such regulations would be more effective for the implementation of the rights and protections under this section.

(3) Irregular work schedules

The Board shall issue regulations for covered employees whose work schedules directly depend on the schedule of the House of Representatives or the Senate that shall be comparable to the provisions in the Fair Labor Standards Act of 1938 that apply to employees who have irregular work schedules.

* * *

Sec. 207 [2 U.S.C. § 1317]. Prohibition of intimidation or reprisal

(a) In general

It shall be unlawful for an employing office to intimidate, take reprisal against, or otherwise discriminate against, any covered employee because the covered employee has opposed any practice made unlawful by this Act, or because the covered employee has initiated proceedings, made a charge, or testified, assisted, or participated in any manner in a hearing or other proceeding under this Act.

(b) Remedy

The remedy available for a violation of subsection (a) shall be such legal or equitable remedy as may be appropriate to redress a violation of subsection (a).

* * *

Sec. 225 [2 U.S.C. § 1361]. General applicable remedies and limitations

(a) Attorney's fees

If a covered employee, with respect to any claim under this Act, or a qualified person with a disability, with respect to any claim under section 210, is a prevailing party in any proceeding under section 405, 406, 407, or 408, the hearing officer, Board, or court, as the case may be, may award attorney's fees, expert fees, and any other costs as would be appropriate if awarded under section 2000e–5(k) of title 42 [Title VII].

(b) Interest

In any proceeding under section 1405, 1406, 1407, or 1408 of this title, the same interest to compensate for delay in payment shall be made available as would be appropriate if awarded under section 717(d) of the Civil Rights Act of 1964 (42 U.S.C. § 2000e–16(d)).

(c) Civil penalties and punitive damages

No civil penalty or punitive damages may be awarded with respect to any claim under this Chapter.

(d) Exclusive procedure

(1) In general

Except as provided in paragraph (2), no person may commence an administrative or judicial proceeding to seek a remedy for the rights and protections afforded by this Act except as provided in this Act.

(2) Veterans

A covered employee under section 206 may also utilize any provisions of chapter 43 of title 38 that are applicable to that employee.

(e) Scope of remedy

Only a covered employee who has undertaken and completed the procedures described in sections 402 and 403 may be granted a remedy under part A of this title.

(f) Construction

(1) Definitions and exemptions

Except where inconsistent with definitions and exemptions provided in this Act, the definitions and exemptions in the laws made applicable by this Act shall apply under this Act.

(2) Size limitations

Notwithstanding paragraph (1), provisions in the laws made applicable under this Act (other than the Worker Adjustment and Retraining Notification Act) determining coverage based on size, whether expressed in terms of numbers of employees, amount of business transacted, or other measure, shall not apply in determining coverage under this Act.

(3) Executive branch enforcement

This Act shall not be construed to authorize enforcement by the executive branch of this Chapter.

* * *

Sec. 301 [2 U.S.C. § 1381]. Establishment of office of compliance

(a) Establishment

There is established, as an independent office within the legislative branch of the Federal Government, the Office of Compliance.

(b) Board of Directors

The Office shall have a Board of Directors. The Board shall consist of 5 individuals jointly appointed by the Speaker of the House of Representatives, the Majority Leader of the Senate and the Minority Leaders of the House of Representatives and the Senate. Appointment of the first 5 members of the Board shall be completed not later than 90 days after the date of the enactment of this Act.

(c) Chair

The Chair shall be appointed from members of the Board jointly by the Speaker of the House of Representatives, the Majority Leader of the Senate, and the Minority Leaders of the House of Representatives and the Senate.

(d) Board of Directors qualifications

(1) Specific qualifications

Selection and appointment of members of the Board shall be without regard to political affiliation and solely on the basis of fitness to perform the duties of the Office. Members of the Board shall have training or experience in the application of the rights, protections, and remedies under one or more of the laws made applicable under section 1302 of this title.

* * *

Sec. 401 [2 U.S.C. § 1401]. Procedure for consideration of alleged violations

Except as otherwise provided, the procedure for consideration of alleged violations of part A of title II consists of—

(1) counseling as provided in section 402;

(2) mediation as provided in section 403; and

(3) election, as provided in section 404, of either—

(A) a formal complaint and hearing as provided in section 405, subject to Board review as provided in section 406, and judicial review in the United States Court of Appeals for the Federal Circuit as provided in section 407, or

(B) a civil action in a district court of the United States as provided in section 408.

In the case of an employee of the Office of the Architect of the Capitol or of the Capitol Police, the Executive Director, after receiving a request for counseling under section 402, may recommend that the employee use the grievance procedures of the Architect of the Capitol or the Capitol Police for resolution of the employee's grievance for a specific period of time, which shall not count against the time available for counseling or mediation.

Sec. 402 [2 U.S.C. § 1402]. Counseling

(a) In general

To commence a proceeding, a covered employee alleging a violation of a law made applicable under part A of title II shall request counseling by the Office. The Office shall provide the employee with all relevant information with respect to the rights of the employee. A request for counseling shall be made not later than 180 days after the date of the alleged violation.

(b) Period of counseling

The period for counseling shall be 30 days unless the employee and the Office agree to reduce the period. The period shall begin on the date the request for counseling is received.

(c) Notification of end of counseling period

The Office shall notify the employee in writing when the counseling period has ended.

Sec. 403 [2 U.S.C. § 1403]. Mediation

(a) Initiation

Not later than 15 days after receipt by the employee of notice of the end of the counseling period under section 402, but prior to and as a condition of making an election under section 404, the covered employee who alleged a violation of a law shall file a request for mediation with the Office.

(b) Process

Mediation under this section—

(1) may include the Office, the covered employee, the employing office, and one or more individuals appointed by the Executive Director after considering recommendations by organizations composed primarily of individuals experienced in adjudicating or arbitrating personnel matters, and

(2) shall involve meetings with the parties separately or jointly for the purpose of resolving the dispute between the covered employee and the employing office.

(c) Mediation period

The mediation period shall be 30 days beginning on the date the request for mediation is received. The mediation period may be extended for additional periods at the joint request of the covered employee and employing office. The Office shall notify in writing the covered employee and the employing office when the mediation period has ended.

(d) Independence of mediation process

No individual, who is appointed by the Executive Director to mediate, may conduct or aid in a hearing conducted under section 405 with respect to the same matter or shall be subject to subpoena or any other compulsory process with respect to the same matter.

Sec. 404 [2 U.S.C. § 1404]. Election of proceeding

Not later than 90 days after a covered employee receives notice of the end of the period of mediation, but no sooner than 30 days after receipt of such notification, such covered employee may either—

(1) file a complaint with the Office in accordance with section 405, or

(2) file a civil action in accordance with section 408 in the United States district court for the district in which the employee is employed or for the District of Columbia.

Sec. 405 [2 U.S.C. § 1405]. Complaint and hearing

(a) In general

A covered employee may, upon the completion of mediation under section 403, file a complaint with the Office. The respondent to the complaint shall be the employing office—

(1) involved in the violation, or

(2) in which the violation is alleged to have occurred,

and about which mediation was conducted.

(b) Dismissal

A hearing officer may dismiss any claim that the hearing officer finds to be frivolous or that fails to state a claim upon which relief may be granted.

(c) Hearing officer

(1) Appointment

Upon the filing of a complaint, the Executive Director shall appoint an independent hearing officer to consider the complaint and render a decision. No Member of the House of Representatives, Senator, officer of either the House of Representatives or the Senate, head of an employing office, member of the Board, or covered employee may be appointed to be a hearing officer. The Executive Director shall select hearing officers on a rotational or random basis from the lists developed under paragraph (2). Nothing in this section shall prevent the appointment of hearing officers as full-time employees of the Office or the selection of hearing officers on the basis of specialized expertise needed for particular matters.

(2) Lists

The Executive Director shall develop master lists, composed of—

(A) members of the bar of a State or District of Columbia and retired judges of the United States courts who are experienced in adjudicating or arbitrating the kinds of personnel and other matters for which hearings may be held under this Act, and

(B) individuals expert in technical matters relating to accessibility and usability by persons with disabilities or technical matters relating to occupational safety and health.

In developing lists, the Executive Director shall consider candidates recommended by the Federal Mediation and Conciliation Service or the Administrative Conference of the United States.

(d) Hearing

Unless a complaint is dismissed before a hearing, a hearing shall be—

(1) conducted in closed session on the record by the hearing officer;

(2) commenced no later than 60 days after filing of the complaint under subsection (a), except that the Office may, for good cause, extend up to an additional 30 days the time for commencing a hearing; and

(3) conducted, except as specifically provided in this Act and to the greatest extent practicable, in accordance with the principles and procedures set forth in sections 554 through 557 of title 5, United States Code.

(e) Discovery

Reasonable prehearing discovery may be permitted at the discretion of the hearing officer.

(f) Subpoenas

(1) In general

At the request of a party, a hearing officer may issue subpoenas for the attendance of witnesses and for the production of correspondence, books, papers, documents, and other records. The attendance of witnesses and the production of records may be required from any place within the United States. Subpoenas shall be served in the manner provided under rule 45(b) of the Federal Rules of Civil Procedure.

(2) Objections

If a person refuses, on the basis of relevance, privilege, or other objection, to testify in response to a question or to produce records in connection with a proceeding before a hearing officer, the hearing officer shall rule on the objection. At the request of the witness or any party, the hearing officer shall (or on the hearing officer's own initiative, the hearing officer may) refer the ruling to the Board for review.

(3) Enforcement

(A) In general

If a person fails to comply with a subpoena, the Board may authorize the General Counsel to apply, in the name of the Office, to an appropriate United States district court for an order requiring that person to appear before the hearing officer to give testimony or produce records. The application may be made within the judicial district where the hearing is conducted or where that person is found, resides, or transacts business. Any failure to obey a lawful order of the district court issued pursuant to this section may be held by such court to be a civil contempt thereof.

(B) Service of process

Process in an action or contempt proceeding pursuant to subparagraph (A) may be served in any judicial district in which the person refusing or failing to comply, or threatening to refuse or not to comply, resides, transacts business, or may be found, and subpoenas for witnesses who are required to attend such proceedings may run into any other district.

(g) Decision

The hearing officer shall issue a written decision as expeditiously as possible, but in no case more than 90 days after the conclusion of the hearing. The written decision shall be transmitted by the Office to the parties. The decision shall state the issues raised in the complaint, describe the evidence in the record, contain findings of fact and conclusions of law, contain a determination of whether a violation has occurred, and order such remedies as are appropriate pursuant to title II. The decision shall be entered in the records of the Office. If a decision is not appealed under section 406 to the Board, the decision shall be considered the final decision of the Office.

(h) Precedents

A hearing officer who conducts a hearing under this section shall be guided by judicial decisions under the laws made applicable by section 102 and by Board decisions under this Act.

Sec. 406 [2 U.S.C. § 1406]. Appeal to the board

(a) In general

Any party aggrieved by the decision of a hearing officer under section 405(g) may file a petition for review by the Board not later than 30 days after entry of the decision in the records of the Office.

(b) Parties' opportunity to submit argument

The parties to the hearing upon which the decision of the hearing officer was made shall have a reasonable opportunity to be heard, through written submission and, in the discretion of the Board, through oral argument.

(c) Standard of review

The Board shall set aside a decision of a hearing officer if the Board determines that the decision was—

(1) arbitrary, capricious, an abuse of discretion, or otherwise not consistent with law;

(2) not made consistent with required procedures; or

(3) unsupported by substantial evidence.

(d) Record

In making determinations under subsection (c), the Board shall review the whole record, or those parts of it cited by a party, and due account shall be taken of the rule of prejudicial error.

(e) Decision

The Board shall issue a written decision setting forth the reasons for its decision. The decision may affirm, reverse, or remand to the hearing officer for further proceedings. A decision that does not require further proceedings before a hearing officer shall be entered in the records of the Office as a final decision.

Sec. 407 [42 U.S.C. § 1407]. Judicial review of Board decisions and enforcement

(a) Jurisdiction

(1) Judicial review

The United States Court of Appeals for the Federal Circuit shall have jurisdiction over any proceeding commenced by a petition of—

(A) a party aggrieved by a final decision of the Board under section 406(e) in cases arising under part A of title II,

(B) a charging individual or a respondent before the Board who files a petition under section 210(d)(4),

(C) The General Counsel or a respondent before the Board who files a petition under section 215(c)(5), or

(D) the General Counsel or a respondent before the Board who files a petition under section 220(c)(3).

The court of appeals shall have exclusive jurisdiction to set aside, suspend (in whole or in part), to determine the validity of, or otherwise review the decision of the Board.

(2) Enforcement

The United States Court of Appeals for the Federal Circuit shall have jurisdiction over any petition of the General Counsel, filed in the name of the Office and at the direction of the Board, to enforce a final decision under section 405(g) or 406(e) with respect to a violation of part A, B, C, or D of title II.

(b) Procedures

(1) Respondents

(A) In any proceeding commenced by a petition filed under subsection (a)(1)(A) or (B), or filed by a party other than the

General Counsel under subsection (a)(1)(C) or (D), the Office shall be named respondent and any party before the Board may be named respondent by filing a notice of election with the court within 30 days after service of the petition.

(B) In any proceeding commenced by a petition filed by the General Counsel under subsection (a)(1)(C) or (D), the prevailing party in the final decision entered under section 406(e) shall be named respondent, and any other party before the Board may be named respondent by filing a notice of election with the court within 30 days after service of the petition.

(C) In any proceeding commenced by a petition filed under subsection (a)(2), the party under section 405 or 406 that the General Counsel determines has failed to comply with a final decision under section 405(g) or 406(e) shall be named respondent.

(2) Intervention

Any party that participated in the proceedings before the Board under section 406 and that was not made respondent under paragraph (1) may intervene as of right.

(c) Law applicable

Chapter 158 of title 28, United States Code, shall apply to judicial review under paragraph (1) of subsection (a), except that—

(1) with respect to section 2344 of title 28, United States Code, service of a petition in any proceeding in which the Office is a respondent shall be on the General Counsel rather than on the Attorney General;

(2) the provisions of section 2348 of title 28, United States Code, on the authority of the Attorney General, shall not apply;

(3) the petition for review shall be filed not later than 90 days after the entry in the Office of a final decision under section 406(e); and

(4) the Office shall be an "agency" as that term is used in chapter 158 of title 28, United States Code.

(d) Standard of review

To the extent necessary for decision in a proceeding commenced under subsection (a)(1) and when presented, the court shall decide all relevant questions of law and interpret constitutional and statutory provisions. The court shall set aside a final decision of the Board if it is determined that the decision was—

(1) arbitrary, capricious, an abuse of discretion, or otherwise not consistent with law;

(2) not made consistent with required procedures; or

(3) unsupported by substantial evidence.

(e) Record

In making determinations under subsection (d), the court shall review the whole record, or those parts of it cited by a party, and due account shall be taken of the rule of prejudicial error.

Sec. 408 [2 U.S.C. § 1408]. Civil action

(a) Jurisdiction

The district courts of the United States shall have jurisdiction over any civil action commenced under section 404 and this section by a covered employee who has completed counseling under section 402 and mediation under section 403. A civil action may be commenced by a covered employee only to seek redress for a violation for which the employee has completed counseling and mediation.

(b) Parties

The defendant shall be the employing office alleged to have committed the violation, or in which the violation is alleged to have occurred.

(c) Jury trial

Any party may demand a jury trial where a jury trial would be available in an action against a private defendant under the relevant law made applicable by this Act. In any case in which a violation of section 201 is alleged, the court shall not inform the jury of the maximum amount of compensatory damages available under section 201(b)(1) or 201(b)(3).

* * *

Sec. 415 [U.S.C. § 1415]. Payments

(a) Awards and settlements

Except as provided in subsection (c), only funds which are appropriated to an account of the Office in the Treasury of the United States for the payment of awards and settlements may be used for the payment of awards and settlements under this Act. There are authorized to be appropriated for such account such sums as may be necessary to pay such awards and settlements. Funds in the account are not available for awards and settlements involving the General Accounting Office, the Government Printing Office, or the Library of Congress.

(b) Compliance

Except as provided in subsection (c), there are authorized to be appropriated such sums as may be necessary for administrative, personnel, and similar expenses of employing offices which are needed to comply with this Act.

(c) OSHA, accommodation and access requirements

Funds to correct violations of section 201(a)(3), 210, or 215 of this Act [relating to public accommodation in the Americans with Disabilities

Act] may be paid only from funds appropriated to the employing office or entity responsible for correcting such violations. There are authorized to be appropriated such sums as may be necessary for such funds.

Sec. 416 [U.S.C. § 1416]. Confidentiality

(a) Counseling

All counseling shall be strictly confidential, except that the Office and a covered employee may agree to notify the employing office of the allegations.

(b) Mediation

All mediation shall be strictly confidential.

(c) Hearings and deliberations

Except as provided in subsections (d), (e), and (f), all proceedings and deliberations of hearing officers and the Board, including any related records, shall be confidential. This subsection shall not apply to proceedings under section 215, but shall apply to the deliberations of hearing officers and the Board under that section.

(d) Release of records for judicial action

The records of hearing officers and the Board may be made public if required for the purpose of judicial review under section 407.

(e) Access by committees of Congress

At the discretion of the Executive Director, the Executive Director may provide to the Committee on Standards of Official Conduct of the House of Representatives and the Select Committee on Ethics of the Senate access to the records of the hearings and decisions of the hearing officers and the Board, including all written and oral testimony in the possession of the Office. The Executive Director shall not provide such access until the Executive Director has consulted with the individual filing the complaint at issue, and until a final decision has been entered under section 405(g) or 406(e).

(f) Final Decisions

A final decision entered under section 405(g) or 406(e) shall be made public if it is in favor of the complaining covered employee, or in favor of the charging party under section 210, or if the decision reverses a decision of a hearing officer which had been in favor of the covered employee or charging party. The Board may make public any other decision at its discretion.

* * *

Sec. 502 [2 U.S.C. § 1432]. Political affiliation and place of residence

(a) In general

It shall not be a violation of any provision of section 201 to consider the—

(1) party affiliation;

(2) domicile; or

(3) political compatibility with the employing office; of an employee[.] * * *

EXECUTIVE ORDER 11246—EQUAL OPPORTUNITY IN FEDERAL EMPLOYMENT

Source: The provisions of Executive Order 11246 of Sept. 24, 1965, appear at 30 Fed.Reg. 12319, 12935, 3 C.F.R., 1964–1965 Comp., unless otherwise noted.

Under and by virtue of the authority vested in me as President of the United States by the Constitution and statutes of the United States, it is ordered as follows:

* * *

Part II. Nondiscrimination in Employment by Government Contractors and Subcontractors

Subpart A. Duties of the Secretary of Labor

Sec. 201. The Secretary of Labor shall be responsible for the administration and enforcement of Part II and III of this Order. The Secretary shall adopt such rules and regulations and issue such orders as are deemed necessary and appropriate to achieve the purposes of Parts II and III of this Order.

Subpart B. Contractors' Agreements

Sec. 202. Except in contracts exempted in accordance with Section 204 of this Order, all Government contracting agencies shall include in every Government contract hereafter entered into the following provisions:

During the performance of this contract, the contractor agrees as follows:

> (1) The contractor will not discriminate against any employee or applicant for employment because of race, color, religion, sex, or national origin. The contractor will take affirmative action to ensure that applicants are employed, and that employees are treated during employment, without regard to their race, color, religion, sex or national origin. Such action shall include, but not be limited to the following: employment, upgrading, demotion, or transfer; recruitment or recruitment advertising; layoff or termination; rates of pay or other forms of compensation; and selection for training, including apprenticeship. The contractor agrees to post in conspicuous places, available to employees and applicants for employment, notices to be provided by the contracting officer setting forth the provisions of this nondiscrimination clause.

(2) The contractor will, in all solicitations or advertisements for employees placed by or on behalf of the contractor, state that all qualified applicants will receive consideration for employment without regard to race, color, religion, sex or national origin.

(3) The contractor will send to each labor union or representative of workers with which he has a collective bargaining agreement or other contract or understanding, a notice, to be provided by the agency contracting officer, advertising the labor union or workers' representative of the contractor's commitments under Section 202 of Executive Order No. 11246 of September 24, 1965, and shall post copies of the notice in conspicuous places available to employees and applicants for employment.

(4) The contractor will comply with all provisions of Executive Order No. 11246 of Sept. 24, 1965, and of the rules, regulations, and relevant orders of the Secretary of Labor.

(5) The contractor will furnish all information and reports required by Executive Order No. 11246 of September 24, 1965, and by the rules, regulations, and orders of the Secretary of Labor, or pursuant thereto, and will permit access to his books, records, and accounts by the contracting agency and the Secretary of Labor for purposes of investigation to ascertain compliance with such rules, regulations, and orders.

(6) In the event of the contractor's noncompliance with the nondiscrimination clauses of this contract or with any of such rules, regulations, or orders, this contract may be cancelled, terminated or suspended in whole or in part and the contractor may be declared ineligible for further Government contracts in accordance with procedures authorized in Executive Order No. 11246 of Sept. 24, 1965, and such other sanctions may be imposed and remedies invoked as provided in Executive Order No. 11246 of September 24, 1965, or by rule, regulation, or order of the Secretary of Labor, or as otherwise provided by law.

(7) The contractor will include the provisions of paragraphs (1) through (7) in every subcontract or purchase order unless exempted by rules, regulations, or orders of the Secretary of Labor issued pursuant to Section 204 of Executive Order No. 11246 of September 24, 1965 [section 204 of this Order] so that such provisions will be binding upon each subcontractor or vendor. The contractor will take such action with respect to any subcontract or purchase order as may be directed by the Secretary of Labor as a means of enforcing such provisions including sanctions for noncompliance: Provided, however, that in the event the contractor becomes involved in, or is threatened with, litigation with a subcontractor or vendor as a result of such direction, the contractor may request the United States to enter into such litigation to protect the interests of the United States.

Sec. 203. (a) Each contractor having a contract containing the provisions prescribed in Section 202 shall file, and shall cause each of his subcontractors to file, Compliance Reports with the contracting agency or the Secretary of labor as may be directed. Compliance Reports shall be filed within such times and shall contain such information as to the practices, policies, programs, and employment policies, programs, and employment statistics of the contractor and each subcontractor, and shall be in such form, as the Secretary of Labor may prescribe.

* * *

Subpart C. Powers and Duties of the Secretary of Labor and the Contracting Agencies

Sec. 205. The Secretary of Labor shall be responsible for securing compliance by all Government contractors and subcontractors with this Order and any implementing rules or regulations. All contracting agencies shall comply with the terms of this Order and any implementing rules, regulations, or orders of the Secretary of Labor. Contracting agencies shall cooperate with the Secretary of Labor and shall furnish such information and assistance as the Secretary may require.

Sec. 206. (a) The Secretary of Labor may investigate the employment practices of any Government contractor or subcontractor to determine whether or not the contractual provisions specified in Section 202 of this Order have been violated. Such investigation shall be conducted in accordance with the procedures established by the Secretary of Labor.

* * *

Subpart D. Sanctions and Penalties

Sec. 209. (a) In accordance with such rules, regulations, or orders as the Secretary of Labor may issue or adopt, the Secretary may:

(1) Publish, or cause to be published, the names of contractors or unions which it has concluded have complied or have failed to comply with the provisions of this Order or of the rules, regulations, and orders of the Secretary of Labor.

(2) Recommended to the Department of Justice that, in cases in which there is substantial or material violation or the threat of substantial or material violation of the contractual provisions set forth in Section 202 of this Order, appropriate proceedings be brought to enforce those provisions, including the enjoining, within the limitations of applicable law, of organizations, individuals, or groups who prevent directly or indirectly, or seek to prevent directly or indirectly, compliance with the provisions of this Order.

(3) Recommended to the Equal Employment Opportunity Commission or the Department of Justice that appropriate proceedings be instituted under Title VII of the Civil Rights Act of 1964.

(4) Recommended to the Department of Justice that criminal proceedings be brought for the furnishing of false information to any contracting agency or to the Secretary of Labor as the case may be.

(5) After consulting with the contracting agency, direct the contracting agency to cancel, terminate, suspend, or cause to be cancelled, terminated, or suspended, any contract, or any portion or portions thereof, for failure of the contractor or subcontractor to comply with equal employment opportunity provisions of the contract. Contracts may be cancelled, terminated, or suspended absolutely or continuance of contracts may be conditioned upon a program for future compliance approved by the Secretary of Labor.

(6) Provide that any contracting agency shall refrain from entering into further contracts, or extensions or other modifications of existing contracts, with any noncomplying contractor, until such contractor has satisfied the Secretary of Labor that such contractor has established and will carry out personnel and employment policies in compliance with the provisions of this order.

(b) Pursuant to rules and regulations prescribed by the Secretary of Labor, the Secretary shall make reasonable efforts, within a reasonable time limitation, to secure compliance with the contract provisions of this Order by methods of conference, conciliation, mediation, and persuasion before proceedings shall be instituted under subsection (a)(2) of this Section, or before a contract shall be cancelled or terminated in whole or in part under subsection (a)(5) of this Section.

[Sec. 209 amended by EO 12086 of Oct. 5, 1978, 43 FR 46501, 3 CFR, 1978 Com., p. 230.]

* * *

Part III. Nondiscrimination Provisions Federally Assisted Construction Contracts

Sec. 301. Each executive department and agency which administers a program involving Federal financial assistance shall require as a condition for the approval of any grant, contract, loan, insurance, or guarantee thereunder, which may involve a construction contract, that the applicant for Federal assistance undertake and agree to incorporate, or cause to be incorporated, into all construction contracts paid for in whole or in part with funds obtained from the Federal Government or borrowed on the credit of the Federal Government pursuant to such grant, contract, loan, insurance, or guarantee, or undertaken pursuant to any Federal program involving such grant, contract, loan, insurance, or guarantee, the provisions prescribed for Government contracts by Section 202 of this Order or such modification thereof, preserving in substance the contractor's obligations thereunder, as may be approved by the Secretary of Labor; together with such additional provisions as the Secretary deems appropriate to establish and protect the interest of the United States in the enforcement of those obligations. Each such applicant shall also undertake and agree (1) to assist and cooperate actively with the Secretary of Labor in obtaining the compliance of contractors and subcontractors with those contract provisions and with the rules, regulations and relevant orders of the Secretary, (2) to obtain and to furnish to the Secretary of Labor such information as the Secretary may require for the supervision of such compliance, (3) to carry out sanctions and penalties for violation of such obligations imposed upon contractors and subcontractors by the Secretary of Labor to Part II, Subpart D, of this Order, and (4) to refrain from entering into any contract subject to this Order, or extension or other modification of such a contract with a contractor debarred from Government contracts under Part II, Subpart D, of this Order.

* * *

FEDERAL ARBITRATION ACT OF 1925
9 U.S.C. §§ 1–7, 9–11

Sec. 1. "Maritime transactions" and "commerce" defined; exceptions to operation of title

"Maritime transactions", as herein defined, means charter parties, bills of lading of water carriers, agreements relating to wharfage, supplies furnished vessels or repairs to vessels, collisions, or any other matters in foreign commerce which, if the subject of controversy, would be embraced within admiralty jurisdiction; "commerce", as herein defined, means commerce among the several States or with foreign nations, or in any Territory of the United States or in the District of Columbia, or between any such Territory and another, or between any such Territory and any State or foreign nation, or between the District of Columbia and any State or Territory or foreign nation, but nothing herein contained shall apply to contracts of employment of seamen, railroad employees, or any other class of workers engaged in foreign or interstate commerce.

Adams p. 929

Sec. 2. Validity, irrevocability, and enforcement of agreements to arbitrate

A written provision in any maritime transaction or a contract evidencing a transaction involving commerce to settle by arbitration a controversy thereafter arising out of such contract or transaction, or the refusal to perform the whole or any part thereof, or an agreement in writing to submit to arbitration an existing controversy arising out of such a contract, transaction, or refusal, shall be valid, irrevocable, and enforceable, save upon such grounds as exist at law or in equity for the revocation of any contract.

Sec. 3. Stay of proceedings where issue therein referable to arbitration

If any suit or proceeding be brought in any of the courts of the United States upon any issue referable to arbitration under an agreement in writing for such arbitration, the court in which such suit is pending, upon being satisfied that the issue involved in such suit or proceeding is referable to arbitration under such an agreement, shall on application of one of the parties stay the trial of the action until such arbitration has been had in accordance with the terms of the agreement, providing the applicant for the stay is not in default in proceeding with such arbitration.

Sec. 4. Failure to arbitrate under agreement; petition to United States court having jurisdiction for order to compel arbitration; notice and service thereof; hearing and determination

A party aggrieved by the alleged failure, neglect, or refusal of another to arbitrate under a written agreement for arbitration may petition any United States district court which, save for such agreement, would have jurisdiction under Title 28, in a civil action or in admiralty of the subject matter of a suit arising out of the controversy between the parties, for an order directing that such arbitration proceed in the manner provided for in such agreement. Five days' notice in writing of such application shall be served upon the party in default. Service thereof shall be made in the manner provided by the Federal Rules of Civil Procedure. The court shall hear the parties, and upon being satisfied that the making of the agreement for arbitration or the failure to comply therewith is not in issue, the court shall make an order directing the parties to proceed to arbitration in accordance with the terms of the agreement. The hearing and proceedings, under such agreement, shall be within the district in which the petition for an order directing such arbitration is filed. If the making of the arbitration agreement or the failure, neglect, or refusal to perform the same be in issue, the court shall proceed summarily to the trial thereof. If no jury trial be demanded by the party alleged to be in default, or if the matter in dispute is within admiralty jurisdiction, the court shall hear and determine such issue. Where such an issue is raised, the party alleged to be in default may, except in cases of admiralty, on or before the return day of the notice of application, demand a jury trial of such issue, and upon such demand the court shall make an order referring the issue or issues to a jury in the manner provided by the Federal Rules of Civil Procedure, or may specially call a jury for that purpose. If the jury find that no agreement in writing for arbitration was made or that there is no default in proceeding thereunder, the proceeding shall be dismissed. If the jury find that an agreement for arbitration was made in writing and that there is a default in proceeding thereunder, the court shall make an order summarily directing the parties to proceed with the arbitration in accordance with the terms thereof.

Sec. 5. Appointment of arbitrators or umpire

If in the agreement provision be made for a method of naming or appointing an arbitrator or arbitrators or an umpire, such method shall be followed; but if no method be provided therein, or if a method be provided and any party thereto shall fail to avail himself of such method, or if for any other reason there shall be a lapse in the naming of an arbitrator or arbitrators or umpire, or in filling a vacancy, then upon the application of either party to the controversy the court shall designate and appoint an arbitrator or arbitrators or umpire, as the case may require, who shall act under the said agreement with the same force and effect as if he or they had been specifically named therein; and unless otherwise provided in the agreement the arbitration shall be by a single arbitrator.

Sec. 6. Application heard as motion

Any application to the court hereunder shall be made and heard in the manner provided by law for the making and hearing of motions, except as otherwise herein expressly provided.

Sec. 7. Witnesses before arbitrators; fees; compelling attendance

The arbitrators selected either as prescribed in this title or otherwise, or a majority of them, may summon in writing any person to attend before them or any of them as a witness and in a proper case to bring with him or them any book, record, document, or paper which may be deemed material as evidence in the case. The fees for such attendance shall be the same as the fees of witnesses before masters of the United States courts. Said summons shall issue in the name of the arbitrator or arbitrators, or a majority of them, and shall be signed by the arbitrators, or a majority of them, and shall be directed to the said person and shall be served in the same manner as subpoenas to appear and testify before the court; if any person or persons so summoned to testify shall refuse or neglect to obey said summons, upon petition the United States district court for the district in which such arbitrators, or a majority of them, are sitting may compel the attendance of such person or persons before said arbitrator or arbitrators, or punish said person or persons for contempt in the same manner provided by law for securing the attendance of witnesses or their punishment for neglect or refusal to attend in the courts of the United States.

* * *

Sec. 9. Award of arbitrators; confirmation; jurisdiction; procedure

If the parties in their agreement have agreed that a judgment of the court shall be entered upon the award made pursuant to the arbitration, and shall specify the court, then at any time within one year after the award is made any party to the arbitration may apply to the court so specified for an order confirming the award, and thereupon the court must grant such an order unless the award is vacated, modified, or corrected as prescribed in sections 10 and 11 of this title. If no court is specified in the agreement of the parties, then such application may be made to the United States court in and for the district within which such award was made. Notice of the application shall be served upon the adverse party, and thereupon the court shall have jurisdiction of such party as though he had appeared generally in the proceeding. If the adverse party is a resident of the district within which the award was made, such service shall be made upon the adverse party or his attorney as prescribed by law for service of notice of motion in an action in the same court. If the adverse party shall be a nonresident, then the notice of the application shall be served by the marshal of any district within which the adverse party may be found in like manner as other process of the court.

Sec. 10. Same; vacation; grounds; rehearing

(a) In any of the following cases the United States court in and for the district wherein the award was made may make an order vacating the award upon the application of any party to the arbitration—

(1) where the award was procured by corruption, fraud, or undue means;

(2) where there was evident partiality or corruption in the arbitrators, or either of them;

(3) where the arbitrators were guilty of misconduct in refusing to postpone the hearing, upon sufficient cause shown, or in refusing to hear evidence pertinent and material to the controversy; or of any other misbehavior by which the rights of any party have been prejudiced; or

(4) where the arbitrators exceeded their powers, or so imperfectly executed them that a mutual, final, and definite award upon the subject matter submitted was not made.

* * *

(b) If an award is vacated and the time within which the agreement required the award to be made has not expired, the court may, in its discretion, direct a rehearing by the arbitrators.

(c) The United States district court for the district wherein an award was made that was issued pursuant to section 580 of title 5 may make an order vacating the award upon the application of a person, other than a party to the arbitration, who is adversely affected or aggrieved by the award, if the use of arbitration or the award is clearly inconsistent with the factors set forth in section 572 of title 5.

Sec. 11. Same; modification or correction; grounds; order

In either of the following cases the United States court in and for the district wherein the award was made may make an order modifying or correcting the award upon the application of any party to the arbitration—

(a) Where there was an evident material miscalculation of figures or an evident material mistake in the description of any person, thing, or property referred to in the award.

(b) Where the arbitrators have awarded upon a matter not submitted to them, unless it is a matter not affecting the merits of the decision upon the matter submitted.

(c) Where the award is imperfect in matter of form not affecting the merits of the controversy.

The order may modify and correct the award, so as to effect the intent thereof and promote justice between the parties.

* * *

EQUAL EMPLOYMENT OPPORTUNITY COMMISSION ENFORCEMENT GUIDANCE: VICARIOUS EMPLOYER LIABILITY FOR UNLAWFUL HARASSMENT BY SUPERVISORS

EEOC Compliance Manual (CCH) ¶ 3116 (June 18, 1999)

* * *

I. Introduction

In *Burlington Industries, Inc. v. Ellerth,* 118 S.Ct. 2257 (1998), and *Faragher v. City of Boca Raton,* 118 S.Ct. 2275 (1998), the Supreme Court made clear that employers are subject to vicarious liability for unlawful harassment by supervisors. The standard of liability set forth in these decisions is premised on two principles: 1) an employer is responsible for the acts of its supervisors, and 2) employers should be encouraged to prevent harassment and employees should be encouraged to avoid or limit the harm from harassment. In order to accommodate these principles, the Court held that an employer is always liable for a supervisor's harassment if it culminates in a tangible employment action. However, if it does not, the employer may be able to avoid liability or limit damages by establishing an affirmative defense that includes two necessary elements:

(a) the employer exercised reasonable care to prevent and correct promptly any harassing behavior, and

(b) the employee unreasonably failed to take advantage of any preventive or corrective opportunities provided by the employer or to avoid harm otherwise.

While the *Faragher* and *Ellerth* decisions addressed sexual harassment, the Court's analysis drew upon standards set forth in cases involving harassment on other protected bases. * * *

* * *

The question of liability arises only after there is a determination that unlawful harassment occurred. Harassment does not violate federal law unless it involves discriminatory treatment on the basis of race, color, sex, religion, national origin, age of 40 or older, disability, or protected activity under the anti-discrimination statutes. * * *

This document supersedes previous Commission guidance on the issue of vicarious liability for harassment by supervisors. The Commission's long-standing guidance on employer liability for harassment by co-workers remains in effect—an employer is liable if it knew or should have known of the misconduct, unless it can show that it took immediate and appropriate corrective action. The standard is the same in the case of non-employees, but the employer's control over such individuals' misconduct is considered.

II. The Vicarious Liability Rule Applies to Unlawful Harassment on All Covered Bases

The rule in *Ellerth* and *Faragher* regarding vicarious liability applies to harassment by supervisors based on race, color, sex (whether or not of a sexual nature), religion, national origin, protected activity, age, or disability. Thus, employers should establish anti-harassment policies and complaint procedures covering all forms of unlawful harassment.

III. Who Qualifies as a Supervisor?

A. Harasser in Supervisory Chain of Command

An employer is subject to vicarious liability for unlawful harassment if the harassment was committed by "a supervisor with immediate (or successively higher) authority over the employee." Thus, it is critical to determine whether the person who engaged in unlawful harassment had supervisory authority over the complainant.

The federal employment discrimination statutes do not contain or define the term "supervisor." The statutes make employers liable for the discriminatory acts of their "agents," and supervisors are agents of their employers. * * *

The Supreme Court, in *Faragher* and *Ellerth*, reasoned that vicarious liability for supervisor harassment is appropriate because supervisors are aided in such misconduct by the authority that the employers delegated to them. Therefore, that authority must be of a sufficient magnitude so as to assist the harasser explicitly or implicitly in carrying out the harassment. The determination as to whether a harasser had such authority is based on his or her job function rather than job title (e.g., "team leader") and must be based on the specific facts.

An individual qualifies as an employee's "supervisor" if:

a. the individual has authority to undertake or recommend tangible employment decisions affecting the employee; or

b. the individual has authority to direct the employee's daily work activities.

1. Authority to Undertake or Recommend Tangible Employment Actions

An individual qualifies as an employee's "supervisor" if he or she is authorized to undertake tangible employment decisions affecting the employee. "Tangible employment decisions" are decisions that significantly change another employee's employment status. * * * Such actions include, but are not limited to, hiring, firing, promoting, demoting, and reassigning the employee. * * *

An individual whose job responsibilities include the authority to recommend tangible job decisions affecting an employee qualifies as his or her supervisor even if the individual does not have the final say. * * * As long as the individual's recommendation is given substantial weight by the final decisionmaker(s), that individual meets the definition of supervisor.

2. Authority to Direct Employee's Daily Work Activities

An individual who is authorized to direct another employee's day-to-day work activities qualifies as his or her supervisor even if that individual does not have the authority to undertake or recommend tangible job decisions. Such an individual's ability to commit harassment is enhanced by his or her authority to increase the employee's workload or assign undesirable tasks, and hence it is appropriate to consider such a person a "supervisor" when determining whether the employer is vicariously liable.

* * *

An individual who is temporarily authorized to direct another employee's daily work activities qualifies as his or her "supervisor" during that time period. Accordingly, the employer would be subject to vicarious liability if that individual commits unlawful harassment of a subordinate while serving as his or her supervisor.

On the other hand, someone who merely relays other officials' instructions regarding work assignments and reports back to those officials does not have true supervisory authority. Furthermore, someone who directs only a limited number of tasks or assignments would not qualify as a "supervisor." For example, an individual whose delegated authority is confined to coordinating a work project of limited scope is not a "supervisor."

B. Harasser Outside Supervisory Chain of Command

In some circumstances, an employer may be subject to vicarious liability for harassment by a supervisor who does not have actual authority over the employee. Such a result is appropriate if the employee reasonably believed that the harasser had such power. The employee might have such a belief because, for example, the chains of command are unclear. Alternatively, the employee might reasonably believe that a harasser with broad delegated powers has the ability to significantly influence employment decisions affecting him or her even if the harasser is outside the employee's chain of command.

If the harasser had no actual supervisory power over the employee, and the employee did not reasonably believe that the harasser had such authority, then the standard of liability for co-worker harassment applies.

IV. Harassment by Supervisor That Results in a Tangible Employment Action

A. Standard of Liability

An employer is always liable for harassment by a supervisor on a prohibited basis that culminates in a tangible employment action. No affirmative defense is available in such cases. * * *

B. Definition of "Tangible Employment Action"

A tangible employment action is "a significant change in employment status." Unfulfilled threats are insufficient. Characteristics of a tangible employment action are:

1. A tangible employment action is the means by which the supervisor brings the official power of the enterprise to bear on subordinates, as demonstrated by the following:

- it requires an official act of the enterprise;
- it usually is documented in official company records;
- it may be subject to review by higher level supervisors; and
- it often requires the formal approval of the enterprise and use of its internal processes.

2. A tangible employment action usually inflicts direct economic harm.

3. A tangible employment action, in most instances, can only be caused by a supervisor or other person acting with the authority of the company.

Examples of tangible employment actions include:

- hiring and firing;
- promotion and failure to promote;
- demotion;
- undesirable reassignment;
- a decision causing a significant change in benefits;
- compensation decisions; and
- work assignment.

Any employment action qualifies as "tangible" if it results in a significant change in employment status. For example, significantly changing an individual's duties in his or her existing job constitutes a tangible employment action regardless of whether the individual retains the same salary and benefits. Similarly, altering an individual's duties in a way that blocks his or her opportunity for promotion or salary increases also constitutes a tangible employment action.

On the other hand, an employment action does not reach the threshold of "tangible" if it results in only an insignificant change in the complainant's employment status. For example, altering an individual's job title does not qualify as a tangible employment action if there is no change in salary, benefits, duties, or prestige, and the only effect is a bruised ego. However, if there is a significant change in the status of the position because the new title is less prestigious and thereby effectively constitutes a demotion, a tangible employment action would be found.

If a supervisor undertakes or recommends a tangible job action based on a subordinate's response to unwelcome sexual demands, the employer is liable and cannot raise the affirmative defense. The result is the same whether the employee rejects the demands and is subjected to an adverse tangible employment action or submits to the demands and consequently obtains a tangible job benefit. Such harassment previously would have been characterized as "quid pro quo." * * * The Supreme Court stated that there must be a significant change in employment status; it did not require that the change be adverse in order to qualify as tangible.

If a challenged employment action is not "tangible," it may still be considered, along with other evidence, as part of a hostile environment claim that is subject to the affirmative defense. * * *

C. Link Between Harassment and Tangible Employment Action

When harassment culminates in a tangible employment action, the employer cannot raise the affirmative defense. This sort of claim is analyzed like any other case in which a challenged employment action is alleged to be discriminatory. If the employer produces evidence of a non-discriminatory explanation for the tangible employment action, a determination must be made whether that explanation is a pretext designed to hide a discriminatory motive.

* * *

If it is determined that the tangible action was based on a discriminatory reason linked to the preceding harassment, relief could be sought for the entire pattern of misconduct culminating in the tangible employment action, and no affirmative defense is available. However, the harassment preceding the tangible employment action must be severe or pervasive in order to be actionable. If the tangible employment action was based on a non-discriminatory motive, then the employer would have an opportunity to raise the affirmative defense to a claim based on the preceding harassment.

V. Harassment by Supervisor That Does Not Result in a Tangible Employment Action

A. Standard of Liability

When harassment by a supervisor creates an unlawful hostile environment but does not result in a tangible employment action, the employer can raise an affirmative defense to liability or damages, which it must prove by a preponderance of the evidence. The defense consists of two necessary elements:

(a) the employer exercised reasonable care to prevent and correct promptly any harassment; and

(b) the employee unreasonably failed to take advantage of any preventive or corrective opportunities provided by the employer or to avoid harm otherwise.

B. Effect of Standard

If an employer can prove that it discharged its duty of reasonable care and that the employee could have avoided all of the harm but unreasonably failed to do so, the employer will avoid all liability for unlawful harassment. * * *

If an employer cannot prove that it discharged its duty of reasonable care and that the employee unreasonably failed to avoid the harm, the employer will be liable. For example, if unlawful harassment by a supervisor occurred and the employer failed to exercise reasonable care to prevent it, the employer will be liable even if the employee unreasonably failed to complain to management or even if the employer took prompt and appropriate corrective action when it gained notice.

In most circumstances, if employers and employees discharge their respective duties of reasonable care, unlawful harassment will be prevented and there will be no reason to consider questions of liability. An effective complaint procedure "encourages employees to report harassing conduct before it becomes severe or pervasive," and if an employee promptly utilizes that procedure, the employer can usually stop the harassment before actionable harm occurs.

In some circumstances, however, unlawful harassment will occur and harm will result despite the exercise of requisite legal care by the employer and employee. For example, if an employee's supervisor directed frequent, egregious racial epithets at him that caused emotional harm virtually from the outset, and the employee promptly complained, corrective action by the employer could prevent further harm but might not correct the actionable harm that the employee already had suffered. Alternatively, if an employee complained about harassment before it became severe or pervasive, remedial measures undertaken by the employer might fail to stop the harassment before it reaches an actionable level, even if those measures are reasonably calculated to halt it. In these circumstances, the employer will be liable because the defense requires proof that it exercised reasonable legal care and that the employee unreasonably failed to avoid the harm. While a notice-based negligence standard would absolve the employer of liability, the standard set forth in *Ellerth* and *Faragher* does not. As the Court explained, vicarious liability sets a "more stringent standard" for the employer than the "minimum standard" of negligence theory.

While this result may seem harsh to a law abiding employer, it is consistent with liability standards under the anti-discrimination statutes which generally make employers responsible for the discriminatory acts of their supervisors. * * * Harassment is the only type of discrimination carried out by a supervisor for which an employer can avoid liability, and that limitation must be construed narrowly. The employer will be shielded from liability for harassment by a supervisor only if it proves that it exercised reasonable care in preventing and correcting the harassment and that the employee unreasonably failed to avoid all of the harm. If both parties exercise reasonable care, the defense will fail.

In some cases, an employer will be unable to avoid liability completely, but may be able to establish the affirmative defense as a means to limit damages. The defense only limits damages where the employee reasonably could have avoided some but not all of the harm from the harassment. * * *

C. First Prong of Affirmative Defense: Employer's Duty to Exercise Reasonable Care

The first prong of the affirmative defense requires a showing by the employer that it undertook reasonable care to prevent and promptly correct harassment. Such reasonable care generally requires an employer to establish, disseminate, and enforce an anti-harassment policy and complaint procedure and to take other reasonable steps to prevent and correct harassment. * * *

There are no "safe harbors" for employers based on the written content of policies and procedures. Even the best policy and complaint procedure will not alone satisfy the burden of proving reasonable care if, in the particular circumstances of a claim, the employer failed to implement its process effectively. If, for example, the employer has an adequate policy and complaint procedure and properly responded to an employee's complaint of harassment, but management ignored previous complaints by other employees about the same harasser, then the employer has not exercised reasonable care in preventing the harassment. Similarly, if the employer has an adequate policy and complaint procedure but an official failed to carry out his or her responsibility to conduct an effective investigation of a harassment complaint, the employer has not discharged its duty to exercise reasonable care. Alternatively, lack of a formal policy and complaint procedure will not defeat the defense if the employer exercised sufficient care through other means.

1. Policy and Complaint Procedure

It generally is necessary for employers to establish, publicize, and enforce anti-harassment policies and complaint procedures. * * *

An employer should provide every employee with a copy of the policy and complaint procedure, and redistribute it periodically. The policy and complaint procedure should be written in a way that will be understood by all employees in the employer's workforce. Other measures to ensure effective dissemination of the policy and complaint procedure include posting them in central locations and incorporating them into employee handbooks. If feasible, the employer should provide training to all employees to ensure that they understand their rights and responsibilities.

An anti-harassment policy and complaint procedure should contain, at a minimum, the following elements:

- A clear explanation of prohibited conduct;
- Assurance that employees who make complaints of harassment or provide information related to such complaints will be protected against retaliation;
- A clearly described complaint process that provides accessible avenues of complaint;
- Assurance that the employer will protect the confidentiality of harassment complaints to the extent possible;
- A complaint process that provides a prompt, thorough, and impartial investigation; and
- Assurance that the employer will take immediate and appropriate corrective action when it determines that harassment has occurred.

The above elements are explained in the following subsections.

a. Prohibition Against Harassment

An employer's policy should make clear that it will not tolerate harassment based on sex (with or without sexual conduct), race, color, religion, national origin, age, disability, and protected activity (i.e., opposition to prohibited discrimination or participation in the statutory complaint process). This prohibition should cover harassment by anyone in the workplace—supervisors, co-workers, or non-employees. Management should convey the seriousness of the prohibition. One way to do that is for the mandate to "come from the top," i.e., from upper management.

The policy should encourage employees to report harassment before it becomes severe or pervasive. While isolated incidents of harassment generally do not violate federal law, a pattern of such incidents may be unlawful. Therefore, to discharge its duty of preventive care, the employer must make clear to employees that it will stop harassment before it rises to the level of a violation of federal law.

b. Protection Against Retaliation

An employer should make clear that it will not tolerate adverse treatment of employees because they report harassment or provide information related to such complaints. An anti-harassment policy and complaint procedure will not be effective without such an assurance.

Management should undertake whatever measures are necessary to ensure that retaliation does not occur. For example, when management investigates a complaint of harassment, the official who interviews the parties and witnesses should remind these individuals about the prohibition against retaliation. Management also should scrutinize employment decisions affecting the complainant and witnesses during and after the investigation to ensure that such decisions are not based on retaliatory motives.

c. Effective Complaint Process

An employer's harassment complaint procedure should be designed to encourage victims to come forward. To that end, it should clearly explain the process and ensure that there are no unreasonable obstacles to complaints. A complaint procedure should not be rigid, since that could defeat the goal of preventing and correcting harassment. When an employee complains to management about alleged harassment, the employer is obligated to investigate the allegation regardless of whether it conforms to a particular format or is made in writing.

The complaint procedure should provide accessible points of contact for the initial complaint. A complaint process is not effective if employees are always required to complain first to their supervisors about alleged harassment, since the supervisor may be a harasser. Moreover, reasonable care in preventing and correcting harassment requires an employer to instruct all supervisors to report complaints of harassment to appropriate officials.

It is advisable for an employer to designate at least one official outside an employee's chain of command to take complaints of harassment. For example, if the employer has an office of human resources, one or more officials in that office could be authorized to take complaints. Allowing an employee to bypass his or her chain of command provides additional assurance that the complaint will be handled in an impartial manner, since an employee who reports harassment by his or her supervisor may feel that officials within the chain of command will more readily believe the supervisor's version of events.

It also is important for an employer's anti-harassment policy and complaint procedure to contain information about the time frames for filing charges of unlawful harassment with the EEOC or state fair employment practice agencies and to explain that the deadline runs from the last date of unlawful harassment, not from the date that the complaint to the employer is resolved. While a prompt complaint process should make it feasible for an employee to delay deciding whether to file a charge until the complaint to the employer is resolved, he or she is not required to do so.

d. Confidentiality

An employer should make clear to employees that it will protect the confidentiality of harassment allegations to the extent possible. An employer cannot guarantee complete confidentiality, since it cannot conduct an effective investigation without revealing certain information to the alleged harasser and potential witnesses. * * *

* * *

e. Effective Investigative Process

An employer should set up a mechanism for a prompt, thorough, and impartial investigation into alleged harassment. As soon as management learns about alleged harassment, it should determine whether a detailed fact-finding investigation is necessary. For example, if the alleged harasser does not deny the accusation, there would be no need to interview witnesses, and the employer could immediately determine appropriate corrective action.

If a fact-finding investigation is necessary, it should be launched immediately. * * *

* * *

f. Assurance of Immediate and Appropriate Corrective Action

An employer should make clear that it will undertake immediate and appropriate corrective action, including discipline, whenever it determines that harassment has occurred in violation of the employer's policy. Management should inform both parties about these measures.

Remedial measures should be designed to stop the harassment, correct its effects on the employee, and ensure that the harassment does not recur. These remedial measures need not be those that the employee requests or prefers, as long as they are effective.

In determining disciplinary measures, management should keep in mind that the employer could be found liable if the harassment does not stop. At the same time, management may have concerns that overly punitive measures may subject the employer to claims such as wrongful discharge, and may simply be inappropriate.

To balance the competing concerns, disciplinary measures should be proportional to the seriousness of the offense. If the harassment was minor, such as a small number of "off-color" remarks by an individual with no prior history of similar misconduct, then counseling and an oral warning might be all that is necessary. On the other hand, if the harassment was severe or persistent, then suspension or discharge may be appropriate.

Remedial measures should not adversely affect the complainant. Thus, for example, if it is necessary to separate the parties, then the harasser should be transferred (unless the complainant prefers otherwise). Remedial responses that penalize the complainant could constitute unlawful retaliation and are not effective in correcting the harassment.

Remedial measures also should correct the effects of the harassment. Such measures should be designed to put the employee in the position s/he would have been in had the misconduct not occurred.

Examples of Measures to Stop the Harassment and Ensure that it Does Not Recur:

- oral or written warning or reprimand;

- transfer or reassignment;
- demotion;
- reduction of wages;
- suspension;
- discharge;
- training or counseling of harasser to ensure that s/he understands why his or her conduct violated the employer's anti-harassment policy; and
- monitoring of harasser to ensure that harassment stops.

Examples of Measures to Correct the Effects of the Harassment:

- restoration of leave taken because of the harassment;
- expungement of negative evaluation(s) in employee's personnel file that arose from the harassment;
- reinstatement;
- apology by the harasser;
- monitoring treatment of employee to ensure that s/he is not subjected to retaliation by the harasser or others in the work place because of the complaint; and
- correction of any other harm caused by the harassment (e.g., compensation for losses).

2. Other Preventive and Corrective Measures

An employer's responsibility to exercise reasonable care to prevent and correct harassment is not limited to implementing an anti-harassment policy and complaint procedure. * * *

An employer's duty to exercise due care includes instructing all of its supervisors and managers to address or report to appropriate officials complaints of harassment regardless of whether they are officially designated to take complaints and regardless of whether a complaint was framed in a way that conforms to the organization's particular complaint procedures. For example, if an employee files an EEOC charge alleging unlawful harassment, the employer should launch an internal investigation even if the employee did not complain to management through its internal complaint process.

Furthermore, due care requires management to correct harassment regardless of whether an employee files an internal complaint, if the conduct is clearly unwelcome. For example, if there are areas in the workplace with graffiti containing racial or sexual epithets, management should eliminate the graffiti and not wait for an internal complaint.

An employer should ensure that its supervisors and managers understand their responsibilities under the organization's anti-harassment policy and complaint procedure. Periodic training of those individuals can help achieve that result. * * *

An employer should keep track of its supervisors' and managers' conduct to make sure that they carry out their responsibilities under the organization's anti-harassment program. * * *

Reasonable preventive measures include screening applicants for supervisory jobs to see if any have a record of engaging in harassment. * * *

Finally, it is advisable for an employer to keep records of all complaints of harassment. Without such records, the employer could be unaware of a pattern of harassment by the same individual. * * *

3. Small Businesses

It may not be necessary for an employer of a small workforce to implement the type of formal complaint process described above. If it puts into place an effective, informal mechanism to prevent and correct harassment, a small employer could still satisfy the first prong of the affirmative defense to a claim of harassment. * * *

* * *

D. Second Prong of Affirmative Defense: Employee's Duty to Exercise Reasonable Care

The second prong of the affirmative defense requires a showing by the employer that the aggrieved employee "unreasonably failed to take advantage of any preventive or corrective opportunities provided by the employer or to avoid harm otherwise." *Faragher,* 118 S.Ct. at 2293; *Ellerth,* 118 S.Ct. at 2270.

* * * Thus an employer who exercised reasonable care as described in subsection V(C), above, is not liable for unlawful harassment if the aggrieved employee could have avoided all of the actionable harm. If some but not all of the harm could have been avoided, then an award of damages will be mitigated accordingly.

A complaint by an employee does not automatically defeat the employer's affirmative defense. If, for example, the employee provided no information to support his or her allegation, gave untruthful information, or otherwise failed to cooperate in the investigation, the complaint would not qualify as an effort to avoid harm. Furthermore, if the employee unreasonably delayed complaining, and an earlier complaint could have reduced the harm, then the affirmative defense could operate to reduce damages.

Proof that the employee unreasonably failed to use any complaint procedure provided by the employer will normally satisfy the employer's burden. However, it is important to emphasize that an employee who failed to complain does not carry a burden of proving the reasonableness of that decision. Rather, the burden lies with the employer to prove that the employee's failure to complain was unreasonable.

1. Failure to Complain

A determination as to whether an employee unreasonably failed to complain or otherwise avoid harm depends on the particular circumstances and information available to the employee at that time. An employee should not necessarily be expected to complain to management immediately after the first or second incident of relatively minor harassment. Workplaces need not become battlegrounds where every minor, unwelcome remark based on race, sex, or another protected category triggers a complaint and investigation. An employee might reasonably ignore a small number of incidents, hoping that the harassment will stop without resort to the complaint process. The employee may directly say to the harasser that s/he wants the misconduct to stop, and then wait to see if that is effective in ending the harassment before complaining to management. If the harassment persists, however, then further delay in complaining might be found unreasonable.

There might be other reasonable explanations for an employee's delay in complaining or entire failure to utilize the employer's complaint process. For example, the employee might have had reason to believe that:

- using the complaint mechanism entailed a risk of retaliation;
- there were obstacles to complaints; and
- the complaint mechanism was not effective.

To establish the second prong of the affirmative defense, the employer must prove that the belief or perception underlying the employee's failure to complain was unreasonable.

a. Risk of Retaliation

An employer cannot establish that an employee unreasonably failed to use its complaint procedure if that employee reasonably feared retaliation. * * * To assure employees that such a fear is unwarranted, the employer must clearly communicate and enforce a policy that no employee will be retaliated against for complaining of harassment.

b. Obstacles to Complaints

An employee's failure to use the employer's complaint procedure would be reasonable if that failure was based on unnecessary obstacles to complaints. For example, if the process entailed undue expense by the employee, inaccessible points of contact for making complaints, or unnecessarily intimidating or burdensome requirements, failure to invoke it on such a basis would be reasonable.

An employee's failure to participate in a mandatory mediation or other alternative dispute resolution process also does not does not constitute unreasonable failure to avoid harm. While an employee can be expected to cooperate in the employer's investigation by providing relevant information, an employee can never be required to waive rights, either substantive or procedural, as an element of his or her exercise of reasonable care. Nor must an employee have to try to resolve the matter with the harasser as an element of exercising due care.

c. Perception That Complaint Process Was Ineffective

An employer cannot establish the second prong of the defense based on the employee's failure to complain if that failure was based on a reasonable belief that the process was ineffective. For example, an employee would have a reasonable basis to believe that the complaint process is ineffective if the procedure required the employee to complain initially to the harassing supervisor. Such a reasonable basis also would be found if he or she was aware of instances in which co-workers' complaints failed to stop harassment. One way to increase employees' confidence in the efficacy of the complaint process would be for the employer to release general information to employees about corrective and disciplinary measures undertaken to stop harassment.

2. Other Efforts to Avoid Harm

Generally, an employer can prove the second prong of the affirmative defense if the employee unreasonably failed to utilize its complaint process. However, such proof will not establish the defense if the employee made other efforts to avoid harm.

For example, a prompt complaint by the employee to the EEOC or a state fair employment practices agency while the harassment is ongoing could qualify as such an effort. A union grievance could also qualify as an effort to avoid harm. Similarly, a staffing firm worker who is harassed at the client's workplace might report the harassment either to the staffing firm or to the client, reasonably expecting that either would act to correct the problem. Thus the worker's failure to complain to one of those entities would not bar him or her from subsequently bringing a claim against it.

With these and any other efforts to avoid harm, the timing of the complaint could affect liability or damages. If the employee could have avoided some of the harm by complaining earlier, then damages would be mitigated accordingly.

VI. Harassment by "Alter Ego" of Employer

A. Standard of Liability

An employer is liable for unlawful harassment whenever the harasser is of a sufficiently high rank to fall "within that class * * * who may be treated as the organization's proxy." *Faragher,* 118 S.Ct. at 2284. In such circumstances, the official's unlawful harassment is imputed automatically to the employer. Thus the employer cannot raise the affirmative defense, even if the harassment did not result in a tangible employment action.

B. Officials Who Qualify as "Alter Egos" or "Proxies"

The Court, in *Faragher*, cited the following examples of officials whose harassment could be imputed automatically to the employer:

- president
- owner
- partner
- corporate officer

VII. Conclusion

The Supreme Court's rulings in *Ellerth* and *Faragher* create an incentive for employers to implement and enforce strong policies prohibiting harassment and effective complaint procedures. The rulings also create an incentive for employees to alert management about harassment before it becomes severe and pervasive. If employers and employees undertake these steps, unlawful harassment can often be prevented, thereby effectuating an important goal of the anti-discrimination statutes.

†